GEORGE ELIOT

GEORGE ELIOT

by ANNE FREMANTLE

DUCKWORTH
3 HENRIETTA STREET
LONDON   W.C.2

HASKELL HOUSE PUBLISHERS Ltd.
Publishers of Scarce Scholarly Books
NEW YORK. N. Y. 10012
1972

HASKELL HOUSE PUBLISHERS Ltd.

Publishers of Scarce Scholarly Books

280 LAFAYETTE STREET

NEW YORK. N. Y. 10012

Library of Congress Cataloging in Publication Data

Fremantle, Anne (Jackson) 1909-
    George Eliot.

    Reprint of the 1933 ed., which was issued as no. 8
of Great lives.
    Bibliography: p.
    1. Eliot, George, pseud., i.e. Marian Evans,
afterwards Cross, 1819-1880.
PR4681.F7 1972   823'.8 [B]   72-3177
ISBN 0-8383-1503-8

Printed in the United States of America

CONTENTS

6   CONTENTS

CHRONOLOGY

1819....November 22nd. Born.

1836....Mother died.

1838....First visit to London.

1840....Poem in *Christian Observer*, signed " M. A. E."

1841.... November 13th. Loses faith.

1842....February. Quarrels with father about going to church.

1843–6..Translating Strauss' *Leben Jesu*.

1848....Translating Spinoza's *Tractatus Theologico-Politicus*.

1849....May 31st. Father dies.

1849....June. Continental tour.

1850....March. Return to England.

1851....January. Review of Mackay's *Progress of the Intellect*, by Marian Evans, in *Westminster Review*.

1851....September. Marian goes to 142 Strand as boarder with Chapmans. Becomes assistant editor of the *Westminster Review*. Meets Herbert Spencer and G. H. Lewes.

1853....October. Begins to live with Lewes.

1854....July. Translation of Feuerbach's *Essence of Christianity*.

1854....July 20th. Went to Continent with Lewes.

1855....April. Returned to London : finished Spinoza.

1856....*Amos Barton.*

1857....*Scenes of Clerical Life.*

1858....*Adam Bede.*

1859....*The Lifted Veil.*

1860....*The Mill on the Floss.*

1861....*Silas Marner.* Visit to Florence.

1862....*Romola.*

1866....*Felix Holt.*

1867....Visits Spain.

1868....*Spanish Gypsy.*

1869....*Brother and Sister* Sonnets.

1872....*Middlemarch.*

1876....*Daniel Deronda.*

1878....G. H. Lewes died.

1879....*Impressions of Theophrastus Such.*

1880....May 6th. Married J. W. Cross.

1880....December 22nd. Died.

CHAPTER I

Ancestors – parents – environment – Mary Ann Evans – her brother and sisters – the first book – the first journey – the first schools – Mary Ann Evans at eight.

FROM Northrop in Flintshire a family named Evans migrated to Staffordshire, some time in the middle of the eighteenth century, and settled in the neighbourhood of Ellaston. There, George Evans, a builder and carpenter by trade, begat two sons : Robert, born in 1773, and Samuel, born a year or so later. These two boys grew up to be very different ; Robert was exceptionally able ; of superb physique, he taught himself not only his father's trade, but also to read and write, and he acquired a wide knowledge of mines and plantations, timber-valuation and measurement, and of all that is essential to the management of large estates, whilst Samuel was religiously inclined and rather lazily inefficient, prospering only when in partnership with his brother. One morning these two found their father drowned in a shallow brook near his home. Coming home drunk he had fallen in the dark and so perished. George Eliot must, as a child, have been deeply impressed by this story of her grandfather's death, which she describes minutely in *Adam Bede*, for death by drowning is the constant end of her characters : Maggie and Tom Tulliver in *The Mill on the Floss*, Tito Melemma in *Romola*, and Grandcourt in *Daniel Deronda* all share George

9

Evans' fate. After their father's death, Robert and Samuel Evans for a time carried on his business together, but Samuel with his dreamy unpractical nature soon left carpentering to become a Methodist, and married the original of Dinah Morris, a Methodist woman preacher of great saintliness. Robert's qualities meanwhile brought him to the notice of Francis Newdigate, a local squire, to whom he became agent in 1799. George Eliot describes the relations between her father and his employer in her account of the friendship between Adam Bede and Arthur Donnithorne, and gives yet another picture of Newdigate in Squire Oldinport, of *Amos Barton*. In 1801 Robert Evans married Harriott Poynton, " friend and servant of the family of Arbury," probably a servant at Arbury Hall, then the seat of Sir Roger Newdigate, uncle to Francis, and founder of the Newdigate prize. By Harriott, Robert Evans had two children, Robert, born in 1802, and Frances Lucy, born in 1805, after he had followed his employer to Kirk Hallam, in Derbyshire. In 1806 at his uncle's death, Francis Newdigate inherited Arbury Hall, and Robert Evans, accompanied by his whole family, migrated with his employer, to settle at Arbury Farm. There, thanks to his employer's excellent opinion of him, Robert Evans became agent to several of the surrounding landowners, and, though he never grew very wealthy, he definitely established himself in the yeoman farmer class, though born a peasant. Harriott Evans died in 1809, and in 1813 her

widower married Christiana Pearson, the original
of both Mrs. Poyser and Mrs. Hackit. She
was a " superior " woman, a cut above her husband both socially and financially, and he went
always rather in awe of her, and of her three
sisters, Mrs. Everard, Mrs. Johnson and Mrs.
Garner, whom their niece was to portray most
unlovingly as the Dodsons. Certainly they
cannot have been easy in-laws for poor Robert
Evans, full as they were of " the traditions of the
Pearson family." Christiana Evans had three
children, Christiana born in 1814, Isaac in 1816,
and finally Mary Ann on November 22nd, 1819 –
just six months after the birth of Queen Victoria.
Robert Evans, unlike his " Methody " brother,
always remained a member of the Church of
England, and Mary Ann was christened at
Chilvers Coton church, when only a week old.
In the March following, Robert Evans junior,
then only seventeen, became agent under his
father, and took over Arbury Farm, with his
sister Fanny to housekeep for him : whilst his
father removed to Griff House with his wife and
the three younger children. Griff was a " charming red brick ivy-covered house " on another part
of the Arbury estate. When his youngest child
was born, Robert Evans was forty-six and a,
strong and well-built man in the prime of life.
It is said of him that once, when two labourers
were waiting for a third to help them lift a heavy
ladder from one haystack to another, he carried it
himself unaided : but, for all his superb physique,

mentally he had the inferiorities and humilities of
the self-educated peasant : he owed his good
fortune, his success, his very livelihood, to the
" gentry " and was beholden to them accordingly,
believing in " the Government " with childlike
simplicity and disliking, with all the fear of the
comfortably well-to-do, all rebellion, privy con-
spiracy and schism. He was only sixteen when the
French Revolution broke out, and George Eliot's
lifelong preference for the *status quo* may very
well have come from her father's reactions against
the " Frenchies." He was content not to see too
much nor too well : the Industrial Revolution had
brought mines, manufactures and factory towns
to rural Warwickshire, and his daughter was on
more than one occasion to describe the closeness
of smiling glebe to slum, but Robert Evans drove
about the green lanes in his pony cart, leisurely,
nor worried himself about franchise nor poor-law
reform. The towns, Nottingham, Nuneaton and
Coventry, were full of poverty and discontent, but
in the 1820's the yeoman farmer and the em-
ployees on big estates, provided the landlord was
kindly and resident, were well cared for and
content. From her father, George Eliot derived
her sense of order, of tradition, of continuity : he
gave to all his children a feeling for the solidity
of the material world, a comfortable realisation of
the gradual improvement, not of individuals, but
of conditions. But whatever of spirituality she had
came from her Uncle Samuel, from whom she
probably inherited too her aching need for

affection and support, spiritual and moral as well as physical. Her mother must have been a little formidable ; even her children, we are told, loved but did not kiss her. She was orderly, efficient, overworked, adoring her only son, approving little Chrissie, with her pretty curls and her tidy ways, but completely failing to comprehend her youngest daughter, whose turbulent entry into the world had left her a delicate woman, who once had been so proud of her strength.

The Warwickshire country in which Mary Ann was to grow for the first twenty years of her life, was, like her parents' position in society, pleasant, central, conservative and unextreme. There were no hills, no forests, no rivers ; chess-board-like, the fields were each bounded by their hedges, the cottages each completed by their garden, the lush meadows watered by a quiet canal, whilst the trim villages clustered each round their church spire : it was a landscape that betokened contented respectability, although perhaps the unkind might call it complacent stagnation. George Eliot was a great believer in the effects of environment, and perhaps she owed more than she knew to the pudding-like placidity of her native landscapes. For, though it is the mountain torrents that sweep away the mighty rocks, it is the deep channels that carry the great ships.

Griff House, with its farmyard around it, was a perfect home for small children, and Chrissie, Isaac and Mary Ann had a singularly delightful childhood. Twice a day the Birmingham–Stamford coach would stop at Arbury gates, and all the inhabitants of the farm, children included, would rush to welcome it, and to stare at the postillions, at their horses and at the sleepy travellers inside. Chrissie was the first to be sent away to school and when at home was too afraid of dirtying her pinafore ever quite to enjoy the same romps as the other two, but Mary Ann would follow Isaac everywhere, adoringly, always happy in his company and miserable only that she was a girl. She once even cut off her horrid long hair that was tortured into curling papers, in the hope of accomplishing thereby a metamorphosis, but it was of no avail, and " Isey " only laughed at her funny appearance, and her mother and the aunts scolded her. She was a clumsy child, not naturally quick with her hands, and must have been rather a trial to her brother, as whenever she threw a ball it seemed inevitably to land in a window, and her mother, whose failing health had obliged her. to send Chrissie to school, was for ever washing up after the tomboyish Mary Ann. Yet she was no tomboy by nature, but only by adoption and imitation, this girl who hated to bait Isey's crooked pins with worms for fear of hurting them, and willingly ate the lesser share of the sandwiches that he might have the greater, and loved to hide away in the old mill and tell herself stories about the fat white spiders who lived there. She loved to drive with her father, sitting quietly between his knees as he meandered round the countryside ; at three or four, her whole universe

was already centred in these two adored men, her
father and her brother. She was always to have
men in her life, men whom she cared for above all
else in the world, and already she found in them
consolation for the rebukes of her mother or her
aunts. But when they failed her – when her father
was out or she had angered Isey – she would go with
her battered wooden doll into the attic, and there,
driving nails into its Sisera-like head, or covering
it with the caresses she longed to bestow on a
worthier object, she would sublimate her misery
through her imagination : the wooden doll became
the hated aunt or adored brother, and little
"Polly," as her father called Mary Ann, would come
down comforted from the loft to enjoy her pudding,
for she was a greedy child and adored pudding.

She was terribly self-conscious. At the age of
four she sat down to play the piano, of which she
did not know a note, in order to impress the servants with a proper respect for her. Although she
was not especially precocious and had, her half-
sister Fanny affirmed, considerable difficulty in
learning to read, she soon grew fond of reading,
and, all her life long, loved and kept the first book
she ever had, one her father gave her : *The Linnet's
Life*, illustrated with woodcuts, of which, charac-
teristically enough, she liked best the one of Mother
Linnet feeding her little ones. But her most vivid
childish memory was not of reading, but of
fishing. One day when she had been left in charge
of her brother's fishing rod, she had gone to sleep
with it in her hands and woke to find a barge

descending on the line and Isaac shouting at her to draw it in : she pulled and found a silvery perch at the line's end, and thus learned, as she wrote some forty years later, that " luck was to glory wed." Until she was five she went to a dame school close to Griff gates, at the cottage of one Mrs. Moore, but after her fifth birthday she was sent to Attleboro, to Miss Lathom's, where Chrissie already was. Here she boarded, although occasionally she returned home to Griff on Saturdays. She was fairly happy, being by far the youngest member of the school and consequently petted and called " little mamma," but littleness has its drawbacks and one of them was the inability to get near the fire in the winter when the bigger children crowded round it, and the consequent agonies of the cold, and another was her terror of the darkness : in her own words, her " soul became a quivering fear," and, for all her life after, something of that nightly terror remained with her, to humiliate and confuse ; she describes pityingly beautiful Gwendolen Harleth suffering the same alarms. She never seems to have been intimate with Chrissie, although she admired her, feeling for her what Dorothea Brooke felt for Celia, or Maggie Tulliver for her cousin Lucy : a sort of awed respect for one whose clothes were always right, whose behaviour was inevitably correct and who found the rules of life, not burdensome restrictions, but delightful patterns.

At Miss Lathom's she began to read in real earnest, and devoured in her holidays the few books there were at Griff : *The Pilgrim's Progress*, Defoe's *History of the Devil*, *Rasselas*, and a stray number of *Joe Miller's Jest Book*, with quotations from which she somewhat surprised her family : these were some of her early favourites. Some kind neighbouring old gentleman, George Eliot told Burne-Jones, used occasionally to bring with him a book for Marian, and one of these was *Æsop's Fables*, wherein the child discovered for herself her first joke, in " Mercury and the Statue Seller." The first joke is always something of an initiation, and when George Eliot was quite an old woman she could still laugh till the tears ran down her face – although ordinarily she laughed rarely – at the memory of Æsop's humour. When she was not yet eight, her sister was lent a volume of *Waverley*, which Mary Ann devoured, but, before she had finished it, it was returned to its owner. Saddened by her loss, she found the best remedy of all, as she herself describes in the motto of the fifty-seventh chapter of *Middlemarch* :

> *In lines that thwart like portly spiders ran*
> *They wrote the tale from Tully Veolan.*

– she wrote her own sequel, beginning from where she had left off, until her parents got back the book for her.

About her seventh year, she went on her first journey ; for a week she and her father and mother travelled through Derbyshire and Staffordshire to stay with Samuel Evans and his wife, and on their way home through Lichfield they
Be

slept at the Swan. This was always a pleasant
memory and gave her a taste for travelling which
she never lost. On their return her father gave her
brother a pony and at first she was overjoyed, then,
as she realised he preferred the pony to her, she
grew bitterly jealous, and hated the animal that
carried him whither she could not follow. This
was the beginning of an estrangement with Isaac
that increased year by year, until it grew so wide
that even death, which restored Maggie to Tom
Tulliver, was unable to effect a real reunion.
Mercifully, perhaps, since Isey no longer cared
" most " for her, she was sent, when aged about
eight, to a new school, larger than that at
Attleboro. This was at Nuneaton and was kept
by a Miss Wallington, and with that removal her
babyhood was at an end.   " Give me a child till
he is seven, and the Devil may have him after " is
said to be a Jesuit axiom, and it was certainly
true of Mary Ann Evans. What she was, emotionally at seven, she would be her life long.
" Her chameleon-like nature," as she herself
called it, had already received its deepest im-
print.   The quietude, the inevitability of the
country, with its infinite succession of unavoidable
sequences, " with the seed-time and the harvest,
the ploughing and the reaping," had imprinted
itself on her subconscious, so that her philosophy,
when she came to formulate one, was concerned
with the necessity of reaping what had first been
sown and with the adjusting of the human being
to the consequences. She believed the sources of

life to be not inward but outward, dependent on environment, hereditary conditions, social traditions and universal laws. As a child she watched those laws in operation and felt humble submission to be the only response possible. She loved the country always, but less for its own sake or for Nature's than for the simplicity of the human beings it produced. A landscape without figures meant little to her, and her favourite painter was Rubens, because, " His are such real men and women, moved by passions, not mincing and grimacing and posing in mere imitations of passions." Yet landscapes were to her always the background of her thoughts and of her people, and when she was sixty she could still write, " I am always made happier by seeing well cultivated land." By the time she was eight, too, her features were fully formed and she had already a seriousness of expression startling for her years. One of her schoolfellows has left it on record that it was impossible to imagine George Eliot as a baby; " it seemed as if she must have come into the world fully developed, like a second Minerva." She herself said, in her *Brother and Sister* sonnets, that these hours were " seed to all my after good," and, though the Abbé Brémond, in his *Inquiétude Religieuse*, states that " L'enfance avait été grise, grise aussi la première jeunesse," it was the grey of dawn, not of a dull afternoon. She had already endured and experienced more than most grown-ups, emotionally ; during the next few years it was the turn of her intellect to awake and realise itself.

CHAPTER II

Miss Wallington's school at Nuneaton – friendship with Miss
Lewis – Miss Franklin's school at Coventry – return home
and mother's death – visit to London – Mrs. Samuel Evans'
visit to Griff – Isaac Evans marries – move to 21 Foleshill
Road, Coventry.

AT Miss Wallington's there were some thirty
boarders, but Mary Ann Evans made friends with
no one of them. She reserved all her affection for
Miss Lewis, the principal governess, an ardent
Evangelical churchwoman, with whom Marian
became very intimate, and who remained her
greatest friend and confidante for some fourteen
years. It was whilst at this school that she got her
first glimmerings of the grown-up political world
which was to affect her greatly and to form the
basis for her novel *Felix Holt*. After the passing of
the great Reform Bill, on the occasion of the elec-
tion for North Warwickshire, the supporters of
the Radical candidate occupied the poll, " constantly interrupted " the numerous Conservative
" plumpers " and prevented their going to the
elections. The Scots Greys were called in, the
Riot Act was read from the Newdigate Arms, both
Mr. Inge and Mr. Newdigate received injuries
" in the discharge of their magisterial duties,"
whilst several misguided individuals were seriously
injured, and one man was killed. Mary Ann
either herself saw or heard directly of this event.
It was while she was at Nuneaton that her talent
for acting first showed itself and she and Isaac

delighted their family every holiday with charades.
Although she was never considered to be a prodigy
nor treated as one, yet her father and mother were
very proud of their clever daughter and decided,
when she was thirteen, to send her to a school
in Coventry, kept by the Miss Franklins, two
daughters of a Baptist minister who had preached
there for many years. He was the prototype of
Rufus Lyon in *Felix Holt,* where his house in
Chapel Yard is described almost exactly. Mary
Ann had the greatest respect for him and for his
daughters, who taught her to write a good hand
and to speak English, for hitherto she had talked
always in the broad dialect to which she was ac-
customed at home and in which both her parents
spoke. Thus she came to English almost as to a
foreign language, which made her use of it singularly forceful and happy, and never slipshod nor
careless, although sometimes we might wish her
style had been more simple and natural. Her
" puritan predilections should have suggested
simplicity to her"; simplicity, however, is the
supreme quality which she not only wholly lacks,
but never seems even to strive for. But it is impossible to be grateful enough to the Miss Franklins for teaching Mary Ann composition and for
helping her to learn to appreciate beauty of form.
Miss Lewis had already introduced her to poetry,
now the Miss Franklins were to begin her musical
education. She was taught the piano and later the
organ by Mr. Simms, the organist of St. Michael's,
Coventry (who in *Middlemarch* is described as

Rosamund's teacher), and no master ever had a
more enthusiastic pupil. Mary Ann adored her
music and gave herself to it completely, and it
moved her more than any other art, but, although
she was easily the best pupil at Miss Franklin's, she
confesses three years after leaving school that she
has " no soul for music " and is a " tasteless person." She was very sensitive about her pla-; ing,
and, after being summoned to the parlour to play
for the entertainment of visitors, would rush up-
stairs to her room and throw herself on the floor
in an agony of weeping, probably because she
realised that however great her affection for
music might be and however competent her
technical mastering of an instrument might be or
become, hers was essentially an unmusical genius.
She was a very virtuous child, whose compositions
were always found to be so excellent that they re-
quired no correction, but were laid aside for the
delight of her mistresses, who perused them again
and again, and the other girls " loved her as much
as they felt they could love one whom they thought
so immeasurably above themselves " ! At the age
of thirteen she was mistaken one day by a caller
for one of the Miss Franklins, and it is to be
feared that she already realised how very plain,
not to say ugly, she was. It must be a terrible
sorrow to be young and unattractive : to look
into the mirror and see a sallow unhealthy face,
with a yellowish skin, straight nose and mouse-
coloured hair, an equine head, too large and heavy
for the short slight body, and large short-sighted

greeny blue eyes ; but at Miss Franklin's
beauty counted for nothing, or rather for less
than nothing, and Mary Ann Evans was not only
the cleverest pupil, best at music, at literature and
composition, and at French and German, for all
of which excellent teachers were provided, but
also the most holy of their pupils. She adopted
enthusiastically the religious observances of her
teachers, although she never joined the Baptists
but remained till her death ostensibly a member
of the Established Church. She conducted
prayer meetings amongst the girls and for three
years led a very strictly religious life, going
through various stages of belief – from Evangelical
she became moderately Calvinistic and then anti-
supernatural, in which character she wore an
" anti-supernatural " cap, which made her plain
features look uglier than ever. She believed absolutely in reincarnation and asceticism, and
suffered all the strivings of her own Dorothea
Brooke, together with " a great longing to become
perfect. . . ." Her three years at Coventry were
absorbing and interesting, if not happy, for
already Mary Ann's heart and head threatened
to be at variance. She longed only for absolute
faith, but found her own shaken by reading Lord
Lytton's *Devereux*, in which an amiable and
virtuous atheist is portrayed, and also by Scott
and Maria Edgeworth, with their Jewish, Moslem
or merely unbelieving heroes and heroines.
Scott influenced her enormously – the renunciation of Fedalma is of the same quality as that of

Minna, and George Eliot's ideals of Duty, and Devotion to " mine own people," are after the pattern of Evan d'Hu's own loyalties. But at the Miss Franklins' she put Scott aside and struggled to conform her adolescent body and mind to the Calvinistic ideal, with the result that, as Brémond has said of her, " La barre puritaine, qui marque ce front, le laissa toujour grave." When she left school in 1835 it was to go home and nurse her mother, who was in failing health. Christiana Evans had spent what was left of her strength in nursing her husband, who had been very ill, and herself died after a long and painful illness, during which she was devotedly nursed by her daughters, in the summer of that year. The following spring, Chrissie married Dr. Edward Clarke, a surgeon practising at Meriden in Warwickshire, and after a " good cry " over the old home, now so broken up (in which Isaac joined her), Mary Ann settled down, at seventeen, to the management of house and farm and father. With her beautiful hands she made cheese in Mrs. Poyser's own dairy, causing one of the said hands to become larger than the other, a fact which in later life caused her no little pride. She " stood sentinel " over damson cheese by the hour, and confessed that sewing " is my staple article of commerce with the hard trader, time," and that her hand's unsteadiness was caused by boiling jellies. She was tidy, economical and practical in the extreme, having little patience with women who cannot make their houses or their men-folk comfortable, and, as a middle-aged woman, in 1863 could still say, "I think after all I like a clean kitchen better than any other room." Yet for all her strenuous house-keeping duties she found time to take up " good works," to visit the poor and to read aloud to them, to organise clothing clubs and to minister to the sick. She also had a master who came regularly from Coventry to teach her German and Italian – ("There seems," she writes to Miss Lewis, " a greater affinity between German and my mind than Italian, though less new to me, possesses ") – and a music master came to her from the same town. She read immensely, mostly books of a religious nature – Wilberforce, Montaigne, Pascal (the *Pensées* was her bedside book), Milner's *Church History*, Young's *Night Thoughts* (a book she then admired greatly, but later was mercilessly to condemn), Keble and Spencer, and Miss Somerville's *Connection of the Physical Sciences*. She dressed herself as unbecomingly as she could, going about looking like " an owl," denied herself laughter and young society, and indeed all relaxation, and her religion, though it gave her comfort of a sort, cut her off from many pleasures that were open to other girls of her class. She could not have been an agreeable companion and one is tempted to be a little sorry for the odious Isaac, who, having come home from school, now gave himself the airs of a pseudo-gentleman, attended race meetings, hunted regularly, affected High Church views, and generally behaved as one might expect a spoilt farmer's cub, posing before

his family as a young "blood," to carry on.
Poor Mary Ann found him godless company,
and he no doubt wearied of her very godliness.
She was terribly lonely, longing, under her for-
bidding exterior and puritan airs, for love and
affection (how surprised a fellow pupil at Miss
Franklin's had been to find on a spare page in a
dictionary an ardent expression of the pious
Miss Evans' real desires!) and hating the ineffec-
tualities of a woman's life. She was marooned
in an intellectual and emotional solitude which
family ties were powerless to approach. "The
Slavery of being a girl" when she had in her
"a man's force of genius" made her realise only
more acutely how alone she was, and, having no
outlet for her activities, she collected knowledge
until she herself confesses that her mind "presents
an assemblage of disjointed specimens of history ;
scraps of poetry picked up from Shakespeare,
Cowper, Milton and Wordsworth ; newspaper
topics, morsels of Addison and Bacon, Latin verbs,
geometry, entomology and chemistry, reviews
and metaphysics, all arrested and petrified and
smothered by the fast-thickening everyday acces-
sion of actual events, relative anxieties, and household cares and vexations." In the *Mill on the
Floss*, George Eliot describes Maggie's attempts to
find escape from her family and her unhappy
love affair, in pitying words which betray how intensely she must have realised the inanity of books,
"and so the poor child," she writes of her own
lost girlhood, "with her soul's hunger and her

illusions of self-flattery, began to nibble at this thick-rinded fruit of the tree of knowledge . . . she set out towards the promised land alone and found it a thirsty, trackless and uncertain journey." At first she had only Miss Lewis to pour her heart out to in very stilted, pompous, pedantic letters, and it is to her she writes of her first visit to London, whither she and Isey went together for a week in August 1838. She was most impressed by Greenwich Hospital and the great bell of St. Paul's, and refused to accompany Isaac to the theatre, preferring to remain alone in her hotel bedroom, reading the Bible. The only thing she bought was Josephus' *History of the Jews*, at the same shop where Isey bought himself a pair of hunting sketches. As a middle-aged woman, she made Philip Wakem warn Maggie Tulliver against such a refusal of enjoyment. " You will be thrown into the world some day," he tells her, " and then every rational satisfaction of your nature, that you deny now, will assault you like a savage appetite." A bitter prophecy which in her own case was a bitterer retrospect. On her return to Griff she writes to Miss Lewis questioning the propriety or lawfulness of oratorio as " an exhibition of talent," and lays down the law anent the reading of novels. Because of her early delight in them and their promises which life had not fulfilled, she turned against them, and, as she was so often to do later, burned what she had adored. " I owe the culprits a grudge for injuries inflicted on myself ; when I was quite a little child I could

not be satisfied with the things around me ; I was
constantly living in a world of my own creation,
and was quite contented to have no companions,
making use of the material novels supplied, for
making my castles in the air." Now, in the in-
tensity of what is known in catholic virgins as
" L'élan eucharistique des vingt ans," she must
pull down those pinnacles and trample them, yet
she consents that classical fiction be read in order
to understand classical allusions. Besides Miss
Lewis, she found a director, albeit one who
proved a rather fragile reed, in the person of her
aunt, Mrs. Samuel Evans, who came to visit
Griff some time early in 1839. Mrs. Evans was in
her way a remarkable woman, but her revivalist
enthusiasm was hard put to it to cope with Mary
Ann's logical questionings and searchings. It was
during this visit of hers to Griff that she told
Mary Ann how, in 1801 or 1802, she had visited a
girl named Mary Voce who was hanged for child
murder, and, from her aunt's description of this·
event, Mary Ann created the plot of *Adam Bede*
When her aunt left, Mary Ann continued to
write to her, in language which the poor woman
must have found hard to understand, complaining
of her " besetments " as she calls them, of which
the chiefest were ambition and " desire insatiable
for the esteem of my fellow creatures " and an
" altogether benumbed soul."

In January 1840 she first appeared in print :
the *Christian Observer* published a poem of hers,
signed only M. A. E., a farewell to this world, which

the editor suspected of heresy, but which Sir
Leslie Stephen dismisses with the remark that it
" shows religious feeling much more distinctly
than poetical power, in which it resembles most
sacred poetry." Early in this same year she
began to make a chart of Ecclesiastical history
which she had planned the previous year, and
which she engaged to finish by " November
next." This chart was designed to give " every
sort of information about the chronology of the
Apostolical and Patristical writings, schisms and
heresies." The Newdigates allowed her to read
in the library at Arbury Hall, and she set to with
great enthusiasm : happily, however, a chart such
as she planned was unexpectedly published by
Seely and Burnside before she had been at work very
long, which put a summary ending to her labours.

In January 1840, Mary Ann and her father went
on a little trip to Derbyshire and Staffordshire,
and here it was she saw, at twenty-one, for the
first time, hills, " albeit the smallest, and those
noblest children of the earth, fine healthy trees."
She went also to Birmingham, to visit Miss
Rawlins, to whom her brother was engaged, and
she heard some Handel and Haydn. She begins
at this time to write to Miss Lewis as " Veronica "
or " fidelity in friendship," she herself having been
given " the very pretty cognomen of Clematis,
which, in the floral language, means mental
beauty." She said she could not find it in her
heart to refuse this name, although she feared " it
was probably intended as a satire." She was at

this time very bored by Griff, and her letters are
full of complaints that her imagination is an
" enemy I must cast down ere I can enjoy peace."
Her brother was about to be married, and she had
secret longings for pretty clothes and the finery of
" ladies," which the sight of the bride's trousseau
and the wearing of a bridesmaid's frock cannot
have made easier to withstand.   Her brother
married during the latter part of 1840, and this,
together with the coming of the railroad, which
naturally greatly affected Mr. Evans' business as
a valuer, led to Mary Ann and her father remov-
ing from Griff to 21 Foleshill Road, Coventry,
where they settled in 1841.   The semi-detached
suburban villa with its piece of garden was a
great change, and she had her now retired father
much more at home and on her hands.   She
writes pathetically to Miss Lewis, whilst asking
her to come for a last visit to Griff, of how " those
scenes have grown in my affections."

Her brother succeeded her father as the
Newdigates' agent, and he and his wife were
left in possession of the old house.   For Mary
Ann, girlhood was over, and the new town life
at Coventry was to be adult in every sense.   Life
was no longer cloud-castle-enchanted, and only
one illusion remained to her, and that was one
she was to lose in the very near future.   Montégut
describes her well at this time : " De petite
condition, et elle était d'une âme élevée, sans
richesse, et elle était intelligente à l'excès, sans
beauté et elle était femme."

CHAPTER III

THE first few weeks at Coventry were occupied in " paying or receiving visits," and in the wider atmosphere of town life Mary Ann began to expand, and writes to Miss Lewis that she is " really crowded with engagements just now." She quickly made friends with their next door neighbour, a Mrs. Pears, sister to Charles Bray, a ribbon manufacturer, whom the Evans' had known slightly in Griff days. Mary Ann and her father met Bray and his wife again at tea with the Pears' in the summer, but the acquaintance does not seem to have been ripened into friendship until the autumn, when she announces one November day in a letter to Miss Lewis that, " I am going, I hope, to-day to effect a breach in the thick wall of indifference behind which the denizens of Coventry seem inclined to intrench themselves, but I fear I shall fail." She did not fail, and the rather lonely summer in which, despite her crowd of engagements, she could write, " I have of late been made *alive* to the fact that I am *alone* in the world," gave way to a delicious autumn, when she confessed that, " if I were a bird, I would fly about the earth seeking successive autumns." After this second meeting with Mr. Bray, Mary Ann became very intimate

with him and with his whole family ; he was
completely absorbed with the study of phrenology,
to which he devoted all his spare time. In
1839 he had published a work on *The Education
of the Feelings*, and in 1841 his most important
work appeared, *The Philosophy of Necessity*, which
was intended to " apply George Combe's scientific
principals to the regeneration of society." In
1836 he had married Caroline Hennell, whose
brother Charles, with a view to confuting Bray's
objections to Christianity, had undertaken to
examine the evidences. The result was a book
entitled *An Enquiry concerning the Origin of Christianity*, which appeared in 1838. This is a remarkable work, considering that Charles Hennell was
completely unacquainted with contemporary
German scriptural criticism and exegesis, for it
foreshadows Renan's *Vie de Jésus* and is written
in a very simple, unambitious way with much
thoughtful reconstruction of the then little known
Essene teachings. This book Mrs. Bray lent to
Mary Ann Evans, who became completely
absorbed by it. She had approached the Brays
almost in a missionary spirit, longing to heal
their gentle, sceptical souls with gospel balm, but
Charles Hennell's *Enquiry* made her realise the
immensity of those far horizons which Miss
Lewis, or Mrs. Samuel Evans, dear, good people
though they were, could never reach.

Mrs. Bray's sister, Sarah Hennell, who was to
become Mary Ann's lifelong friend, was also
a religious speculator, although she always

remained a deist, and wrote a three volumed work entitled *Present Religion as a Faith owning Fellowship with Thought*, in which she expounded her doctrines. Into this charming family Mary Ann, or rather Marian as she now preferred to call herself, was received with open arms. The first visit was followed by a great many others, and, as they sat about in the drawing-room of Rosehill, the Bray's charming house, discussing the divinity of Jesus and the necessity of belief, Marian's faith weakened. The reading of the *Enquiry* marked a turning point in her life ; she had already lost her childish dreams, she had tamed her imagination ; now she was to slough her faith. On November 13th, 1841, only eleven days after her first visit to Rosehill, she writes to Miss Lewis: "My whole soul has been engrossed in the most interesting of all enquiries for the last few days, and to what result my thoughts may lead, I know not, possibly to one that will startle you : but my only desire is to know the truth, my only fear to cling to error." M. Brémond thinks she can never have experienced any feeling of a truly religious nature, or she would not have passed so peacefully through her crisis, nor written of it so calmly both at this time and later, when she speaks of the " egoism of young cravings," but it is more likely that she had outgrown the narrow intellectual limitations of Evangelical Christianity and was not sorry to discard its tenets. The spiritual adventure of religion never seems to have attracted her, certainly, and mysticism of any sort

CE

was foreign to her temperament. For her, religion was a system of ethics, and, as such, an unnecessarily limited system : her wide charity and her soaring intelligence rejected its barriers Faith, in the theological meaning of the word, she never had : Hennell's *Enquiry* merely removed her beliefs. Yet all her life she was rather sentimentally and wistfully to regret her shrines, and of her, as of Renan, it might well be said that " sa vie fut gouvernée par une foi qu'elle n'avait plus." Her religion was morality, as it was that of the majority of her contemporaries, but, unlike many of them, she seems to have been incommoded by the lack of " something above and beyond science and ethics." Her agnosticism made an immense difference both to her life and, above all, to her writings. Forced to provide for and from herself the moral laws usually attributed to providence, she laboured under a burden oi gravity, of conscience and earnestness, compared with which Christian's load was of feathers. In denying the Kingdom of Heaven she lost the power of wonder – the childlike acceptance of the spiritual as real, which characterises her con-temporaries, Turgeniev and George Sand, and gives to their writings a light and a subtle aroma, a width of vision, which is absent in George Eliot. Since she could not accept the laws of the universe as divine, she must explain them as ethical, in the absence of the Deity she must continually be invigilating the workings of the machine, and in all her actions and her writings she clung to an

inexorable and unavoidable law of consequences,
of inevitable causation and retribution, as the
justification of her absolute ideal of Duty. But
this new Credo of retribution, consequences and
moral duties, was to be built up slowly on the
foundations of the Evangelical temple which the
Brays so conspicuously helped to destroy. For
the moment, the immediate difficulty was a very
practical one for Marian : she had lost her faith,
she could therefore no longer accompany her
father to Mattins. This decision produced a
terrible upheaval. Mr. Robert Evans, to whom
the Established Church and Morning Service
were part of the very bedrock of life, felt this
refusal to be a terrible and inhuman monstrosity.
He went so far as to put his house in the hands of
agents, intending to sell it and to go and live with
Chrissie, whilst Marian decided to go to Leaming-
ton, and there to try and support herself by teaching. Mrs. Pears gallantly offered to accompany
her. Happily, before any such desperate steps
were taken, Marian went off to Griff and
stayed for three weeks with her brother and his
wife. There she thought over her impetuous
conduct, and the glamour of being a martyr,
seeking to free Truth's Holy Sepulchre (as she
put it) from a usurped domination, faded. The
Brays wrote and suggested that social relations
were based on mutual concessions and hypocrisy,
and chided her for making her old father
unhappy ; her brother and Miss Rebecca
Franklin helped to persuade Mr. Evans to take

back his daughter and to withdraw his house from the agents' hands. She agreed to go to church as before, and returned to Coventry, where her life resumed its normal course. In later life she expressed great regret for this episode, which, with a little less impetuosity, and a little careful management, might have been avoided, although she could never, she said, blame herself entirely for it.

Her life at Coventry was now very full and interesting. The Brays' house was a second home, and there she met their many interesting friends, teased Mr. Bray, was playfully affectionate to his wife, and argued learnedly with Sarah. Then the gifted Charles Hennell arrived on the scene ; aged about thirty, very good looking and charming, he was profoundly interested in the highly intelligent girl who had been so impressed by his book. There were the Sibrees too, the father was an Evangelical minister, the son, John, went to a German university, and translated Hegel's *Philosophy of History.* He was one of Marian's correspondents at the time, and the tone of their letters implies that the level of intelligence in Coventry was at that time a singularly high one. To John's sister, Mary, Marian gave lessons in German, and " talked to her freely on all subjects, without attempting directly to unsettle her Evangelical beliefs." The Sibree parents do not seem to have been afraid of the young agnostic, and Mary, later Mrs. John Cash, remained one of George Eliot's lifelong friends. Twice a week

Marian taught her German, and, whilst reading
Wallenstein with her, Mary Sibree one day exclaimed on how life-like the characters seemed :
"Don't say seemed," retorted Marian, "we know
that they are true to life," and she immediately
began repeating the talk of the local labourers,
farriers, butchers and others of that class, with such
close imitation that her pupil was quite surprised
– an indication that nothing was lost to Marian's
receptive mind. Besides teaching, Marian was
learning, Greek and Latin with the Rev. T.
Sheepshanks, headmaster of the Coventry Gram-
mar School, French, German and Italian under
Signor Brezzi, and she was delighted to be near
Mr. Simms, her beloved music master. Her new
friends supplanted her old ; there are no letters
to Miss Lewis after the breach with her father,
and her "crude state of free thinking" had
already alienated Mrs. Samuel Evans. In later
years George Eliot went once to see her aunt,
but "the only result was a very painful inter-
view."

Marian and the Brays made delightful summer
excursions to Wales, to the lakes and to Stratford
and Malvern, accompanied by Charles and Sarah
Hennell. In July 1843 they went, this time accompanied also by Rufa Brabant, daughter of Dr.
Brabant, of Devizes, on a fortnight's tour, visiting
Tenby amongst other places. Rufa Brabant had
been commissioned by Mr. Joseph Parkes, of
Birmingham, and a group of friends and fellow
subscribers, to translate into English Strauss'

Leben Jesu, which had appeared in 1843. But she became engaged to Charles Hennell on the Tenby trip, and in November of that year married him, bequeathing her work to Marian, who undertook it somewhat unwillingly. After Rufa's wedding, she went to stay for a few weeks with Dr. Brabant, to " take his daughter's place "; but this visit was not at all successful, and indeed Dr. Brabant was somewhat scathingly described by Marian in a letter as " the German Professor, Dry-as-dust," and he shares with Mark Pattison the doubtful honour of being the original oi Casaubon.

Marian began her translation in January 1844 and pegged away at it, doing her six pages a day. It was a grim undertaking, and she was often discouraged, confessing herself, " Strauss sick," and bemoaning the fact that she will have him on her hands for a lustrum instead of a year. But her life was by no means monotonous ; at the Brays' she met Robert Owen, who did not impress her, " if his system succeeds it will be in spite of him," and also Emerson, whom she affirms to be " the first *man* I ever met." She considerably surprised this writer by telling him that Jean Jacques Rousseau's *Confessions* was her favourite book, although his rejoinder, that he " shared her preference," is to us no less surprising.

The little holiday trips with the Brays continued, and in July 1844 they went to the lakes, and in April 1845 to Atherstone Hall, where Marian met Harriet Martineau for the first time.

Miss Blind, in her admirable Life, tells how, about
this time, Marian met at the house of her married
half-sister, Fanny, a young artist to whom she
became engaged. But her father would have
none of it, and being a virtuous girl, and not
wishing again to quarrel with him, Marian broke
off the engagement in a letter. The young man's
subsequent career was such, we are told, that
George Eliot may be considered to have had a
lucky escape. Whether she regretted her romance
we shall never know, except that she wrote the
tragic history of Maggie Tulliver, and, through
her, perhaps, bitterly repented her own obedience.

By the beginning of 1846 she was feeling very
depressed and overworked ; " leathery Strauss "
took it out of her terribly, and she had to teach
herself a great deal of Hebrew (of which she was
afterwards very glad, though at the time it was
merely hard work). Miss Hennell was very helpful, reading heroically through the manuscript
and correcting the proof sheets. But, as Mrs.
Bray wrote to her sister, " it makes Marian
ill, dissecting the beautiful story of the crucifixion,
and only the sight of the Christ's image makes her
endure it." (This "image" was an ivory stat-
uette of the Thorwaldsen Christ which stood on
the desk in her study.) " Poor thing, " Mrs.
Bray continues, " I do pity her sometimes, with
her pale, sickly face and dreadful headaches, and
anxiety too about her father." This curious
contradiction – the finding of comfort in the very

image she was destroying by her work, after having destroyed it in her life, is the first indication of the sequence of contradictions which continues all through George Eliot's life. Always her code of life was directly negatived by her way of living ; there has hardly ever been a person in whom " the inconsistency of her conspicuous life with her conspicuous word " has been more marked. It would seem that her heart and her head were at continual variance, in open and incessant conflict ; her showing off as a child to impress the servants and her fits of hysterical tears after being made to play in public at school, her sullen behaviour and her intentness only on excelling at her work, combined with her passionate adoration for Miss Lewis and her longings for love and friendship confided to the front page of a dictionary, the fleeing from all amusement and all beauty, whilst confessing to a great desire to impress her fellow creatures and to gain admiration ; all these were incipient manifestations of the same strange duality. So far as her work was concerned her intellect won, and George Eliot followed only too implicitly the advice of Emerson : " See that you hold yourself fast by the intellect." But her life broke free, despite curb and bearing rein, making her one of the most interesting, as well as one of the greatest, of Victorians.

In October 1845 the Brays, Sarah Hennell and Marian had a delightful fortnight in Scotland ; on their return Strauss was taken up again –

there had been some difficulty about cash, the original subscribers had forgotten their promises or withdrawn from them ; however, Mr. Joseph Parkes remained faithful, he and Mr. Charles Hennell collected £300, and, at last, at the beginning of April 1846, the work was done : Marian writes happily to Sarah, " next week we will be merry and sad, wise and nonsensical, devout and wicked together." The translation appeared in June, published by Chapman, without the translator's name appearing. Her only financial reward was £20, a very strange, meagre result for nearly three years' work, but Strauss wrote her a flattering and grateful letter and contributed a preface. The book was well reviewed and the translation commended, although the translator was spoken of as " a discerning and well informed theologian," which must have amused Marian and her Coventry friends !

The autumn of 1846 was a singularly happy one for Marian and her father. On their return from a visit to Dover, Mrs. Bray writes that Marian " looks very brilliant just now. We fancy she must be writing her novel." The editors of her *Early Essays*, which were privately printed in 1919, consider that " it is morally certain that George Eliot, in the autumn of 1846, was experimenting in literature." It was probably at this time that she wrote the "preliminary chapter" which she found in an old exercise book, in Berlin, and read aloud to George Henry Lewes in 1856. She may, too, have had in mind some original work on the lines of Strauss : she was also reading George Sand with great enthusiasm : " I should never dream of going to her writings as a moral code or text book, I don't care whether I agree with her about marriage or not . . . it is sufficient for me that I cannot read six pages of hers without feeling that it is given to her to delineate human passion and its results so that one might live a century with nothing but one's own dull faculties and not know so much as those six pages would suggest." She read the *De Imitatione* too, and wrote that it made her want to be a saint " for a few months," whilst Sir Charles Grandison was " another delight " : " the morality is perfect, there is nothing to correct." She wrote dozens of ten-, sometimes twenty-page letters, and all these things, " both outward and inward, have contributed to make this November far happier than the last. All the world is bathed in glory and beauty to me now." She paid visits throughout 1847 to Griff, to the Isle of Wight, and to London, where she heard " I Puritani " and Mendelssohn himself, conducting the " Elijah." She carried on long correspondence with John Sibree anent Louis Blanc, Lamartine and French politics. For Blanc she had the greatest admiration, and was inclined to think herself a Radical, but only so far as *French* politics were concerned. In 1848 her troubles began again : during a visit to St. Leonards her father became seriously ill. He had been " poorly " for some time, and it soon became fairly evident that he was not likely to recover. Marian nursed him devotedly, but it was a very trying time for her : as, though he could eat and sleep fairly well, he was entirely incapable of amusing himself, and Marian spent long hours reading the Waverley novels to him. She felt very despairing, and wrote to Sarah that her life was "a perpetual nightmare, always haunted by something to be done, which I have never the time, or rather the energy to do." In March 1849, however, she reviewed Froude's *Nemesis of Faith* in the *Coventry Herald,* and received a most charming note from Froude " naïvely and prettily requesting her to reveal herself." He said he recognised her hand in the review, for they had met at Rosehill, and this encouragement to her first piece of literary criticism was a very welcome " episode in her dull life." She began now to translate Spinoza's *Tractatus Theologico-Politicus,* and found this sombre undertaking well suited to her dismal surroundings and mode of life. At last, on May 31st, her father died, her brother being with her at Rosehill, and she wrote to the Brays : "What shall I be without my father? It will seem as if a part of my moral nature were gone." She was thirty now and her youth was over : she was left with a very small annuity of £80 to a £100 a year and a few very good friends.

Intellectually she had reached her full stature. Her first fervour of agnosticism had given place to a large sympathy : her philosophy was now a humble submission to the universal laws of the

universe, a profound love of humanity, and a
renunciation of all personal and selfish desires,
from an altruistic devotion to the good of the
race. She applied her beliefs to morals and regarded good and evil as the results of man's
environment and heredity and choice, as relative
only and not absolute. Emotionally she had sub-
mitted all her feelings to a controlled and general
affection : she felt deeply all traditional ties, such
as her duty to her father, and was admirably
loyal to them. Her friendships were very passionate, unselfish and sincere : whether the Romieus'
story of her having her head shaved to satisfy
Mr. Bray's passion for phrenology is actually true
or not, it is certainly very typical of her unswerv-
ing devotion. Already, in 1845, she had written to
Sarah : " It seems as if my affections were quietly
sinking down to temperate, and I every day seem
more and more to value thought rather than feeling. I do not think this is man's best estate, but
it is better than what I have sometimes known."
Better perhaps than the next few difficult years,
when for the first and almost the only time in her
life, she was to be practically alone, standing
without support, and was to run the gauntlet of
her own feelings.

CHAPTER IV

Travels abroad with the Brays – visit to Geneva – return to England and life at Rosehill – articles for the *Westminster* – goes
to board in Strand with Chapman – meets Herbert Spencer
and George Henry Lewes.

HAPPILY, the Brays had planned a trip abroad for
June 1849, and the now orphaned Marian accompanied them. They went first to France : to Paris,
Lyons, Avignon, and then into Italy, to Genoa,
Milan, Como, Lago Maggiore, and arrived
finally at Geneva. We do not know what the priggish, Strauss-fed, thirty-year-old spinster thought
of all the beauty that she now saw for the first
time : after a lifetime of Nuneaton and Coventry
it must have been overwhelming, even to her in
her benumbed condition. Certain it was that
when they arrived at Geneva and the question of
the return home arose, Marian decided to stay in
Switzerland. The wise Brays appauded her re-
solve and helped to install her in the " Campagne
Plongeon," a pleasant, " good-sized, gleaming
white house," with a magnificent view of the lake
and the Jura. Here, in this pleasant pension,
she remained for three months, and her letters
" home " to the Brays are very different from her
despairing appeals to Sarah Hennell, written such
a very few months before. The other people in
the pension amused and delighted her, and for
all her ugliness she made friends easily enough.
The Swiss landlady even tried to improve her

appearance. " She has abolished all my curls, and made two things stick out on each side of my head like those on the head of the Sphinx. All the world says I look infinitely better, though I myself seem uglier than ever, if possible." She gave up all attempts to continue Spinoza, and took walks, played the piano, read Voltaire, talked, and attended the lectures of Professor De la Rive on " Experimental Physics." She gave herself completely up to the atmosphere of the little pension and set herself the difficult task of learning to be happy : " One has to spend so many years in learning to be happy," she had sighed at Rosehill, but now boasts, " I am just beginning to make some progress in the science." She begs Mrs. Bray to " pray that the motto of Geneva may become mine : *post tenebras lux*." She wrote letters furiously, as though to prevent herself becoming completely ensnared by the lotus-eating existence of the Genevese boarding-house. " You know, or do not know," she tells the Brays, " that my nature is so chameleon-like, I shall lose all my identity unless you keep nourishing the old self with letters." In October she moved to lodgings in the house of a Monsieur and Madame D'Albert Durade. He was a painter, and they were both gifted, artistic people who made a real friend of their boarder and remained faithful to her even after her " lapse." M. D'Albert Durade translated her books into French, without, in the first instance, knowing that the author of *Adam Bede* was his old guest. While she was staying there

he painted her portrait in oils, and she too painted
his portrait, but in words, for he is the original of
Philip Wakem in *The Mill on the Floss*, and Philip's
sage counsels to Maggie were doubtless first given
to Marian Evans. Himself an oldish man, he
was distressed that anyone so young could be so
sorry and so lonely, and Marian derived from him
much strength and support, both of which she
badly needed at this juncture. It is not easy to
begin life at thirty, to start earning one's living
when one is poor and very plain and no longer
young, but during the whole of those eight months
in Geneva, thanks to the friends she made, Marian
worried not at all about the future but enjoyed
fully each and every day. " The perpetual presence of all this beauty has somewhat the effect
of mesmerism or chloroform. I feel sometimes
as if I were sinking into an agreeable state of
numbness on the verge of unconsciousness," she
wrote. In March 1850, she felt she must return
to England and face the new life that was waiting
for her there, so she set off accompanied by
M. D'Albert Durade, with whom she crossed the
Jura in sledges, and said good-bye to him in
Paris. On her return to England she was at first
very depressed. " Oh, the dismal weather and the
dismal country and the dismal people," she ex-
claims. She was none too sanguine about the
future, and her plans were very vague : " The
only ardent hope I have for my future life is to
have given me some woman's duty – some possibility of devoting myself where I may see a daily

result of pure calm blessedness in the life of another." A noble, womanly aspiration, but hardly an ideal to be expected from a writer whom Lord Acton could seriously pinnacle above Dante, Sophocles and Cervantes.

At first she visited relations, but quickly realised, in spite of their kindness to her, the impossibility of settling down with any of them. Not for her the rôle of poor relation or maiden aunt – she could not bear it. Once again the Brays came to the rescue : she must live at Rosehill with them, they would hear of no other plan. Marian, although she had been enquiring of Sarah about " Mr. Chapman's prices for lodgers, and if you know anything of other boarding-houses in London," was glad enough to accept their offer. And so, for the next sixteen months, Rosehill became her home. Here she wrote her first article : a review of Mackay's *Progress of the Intellect*, which Chapman accepted for the *Westminster*. It appeared unsigned, as did all reviews in those days, but as Mackay was Chapman's assistant editor it was a great compliment to Marian that she was chosen to review this book. Chapman and Mackay visited Rosehill in the autumn of 1850, and when Marian came to London on a visit, in 1851, she stayed at Chapman's house in the Strand. Her host found her " friendly, but formal and studied," and it is to be supposed that the Bohemian, happy-go-lucky atmosphere of that strange boarding-house must at first have somewhat surprised if not shocked her, used as she was to the more formal, provincial and correctly middle-class atmosphere of Coventry. John Chapman was a curious creature : born in Nottingham, he had run away from home to Australia, then come back to England to study medicine, and had given that up for publishing. He was now contemplating the purchase of the *Westminster Review*, which he finally bought in June 1851 for £350. This paper had been founded in 1824 by Jeremy Bentham as the organ of the Radical party, afterwards incorporating the *London Review* and having John Stuart Mill as its editor. Many distinguished Victorians contributed to it : Carlyle, Lytton, Leigh Hunt, Harriet Martineau, and G. H. Lewes. After Chapman took it over, its chief lights were Froude, Frederick Harrison, Pater and Mark Pattison. W. Hale White, who later went on to the staff, found the violently anti-religious tone of the paper very tiresome, and indeed John Chapman seems to have been very aggressive in all his undertakings. The *Westminster* was definitely Positivist, and served as platform for Comte's doctrines.

Marian remained at the Chapmans till March, and, as she became more familiar with this Bohemian household, her relations with the *Westminster's* editor became more intimate. It is difficult to say how far Mrs. Chapman's jealousy of Marian had reasonable foundations, but Yale University possesses, amongst other George Eliot papers recently presented by Mr. Gabriel Wells, a diary of John Chapman's for the year 1851.

DE

This contains detailed descriptions of his relations
with Marian Evans, whilst in a later volume –
for 1860 – he only refers to her occasionally as
"Mrs. Lewes." According to the diary she arrived
in London on January 8th, and a month later
Chapman is commending her " beauty of spirit "
and praising her for being an agreeable companion " although sometimes rude." She remained at 142 Strand until March, and on Mon-
day, 24th, there is the following entry : " M.
departed to-day. I accompanied her to the railway. She was very sad and made me feel so.
She pressed me for some intimation of the state of
my feelings " (here two lines are scratched out in
black ink). "At this avowal she burst into tears. I
tried to comfort her and reminded her of the dear
friends and home she was returning to, but the
train whirled her away, very, very sad. Susanna
was much excited to-day and perplexed with her
packing. She reproached me, and spoke very
bitterly about M." Marian returned to her
Brays, but there was no break with Chapman, for
on April 4th his diary records, " Received from
Miss Evans Susanna's letters concerning her,
which I sent her to read, the bitter injustice of
which caused her to decline doing the Catalogue "
(a *Catalogue Raisonné* of Philosophical Literature
which Cross mentions her having done for the
Westminster), " but she afterwards wrote agreeing
to do it, conditionally that she receive no remun-
eration." On April 5th Chapman wrote to her
begging her to " be calm, and not to let recent

circumstances agitate and needlessly pain her."
In May he went down to Coventry, arriving at
6 p.m. on the 28th, after an exhausting day in
town, during which he suffered toothache, faint-
ness and " dreadful insubordination amongst the
servants . . . disobeying Elizabeth especially."
He found Miss Evans at Rosehill and also Mrs.
Thornton Hunt, the wife of the editor of the *Leader*,
a literary paper run on much the same lines as the
Westminster. Chapman walked next day with M.
before breakfast, told her the exact condition of
things with regard to E., "whom, on every account,
I wish to stay at the Strand. She was much
grieved and expressed herself prepared to atone
in any way she could for the pain she had caused,
and put herself in my hands, prepared to accept
any arrangement I may make, either for her return
to the Strand or to any home in London I may
think suitable in October. She agreed to write the
article on foreign literature for each number of
the *Westminster*, which I am very glad of." During the whole of his stay at Rosehill, which lasted
until June 9th, " M." is mentioned daily, and on
the 8th Chapman notes : " Talked with Bray
about the pecuniary arrangement with Marian
E." On June 16th he complains his birthday was
" made wretched by Elizabeth's positive assurance that she would not live in the Strand after
Miss Evans came to London. This step would be
fatal " (and then follow two more deleted lines).
On July 12th " Elizabeth consented to meet Miss
Evans as a visitor to the Strand." Marian had

come to London to the Great Exhibition, and it was on this occasion that she met Herbert Spencer, who was to be one of the greatest influences in her life. From London she went down to Devonshire, and on August 13th we read, in Chapman's diary, that she and Mrs. Bray arrived from Devonshire, that Chapman met them at the railway station and spent the evening with them at Miss Marshall's. On August 14th, " Elizabeth acquiesces Miss Evans return to the Strand for residence during the winter, which at once cuts a difficulty in two and increases my respect for her." Marian remained as a boarder with the Chapmans until 1853, and, as there are no more intimate or indiscreet entries in Chapman's diary, it is safe to assume both had learnt prudence. It certainly does not do her credit that she returned to 142 Strand in August after her experience of it the previous spring, but any impropriety in her conduct was committed in ignorance rather than of malice prepense. Chapman was a notorious philanderer and at the best of times did not get on with his wife, who, it must be admitted in fairness to him, was a bad cook and of a nagging and jealous disposition. He made love to Marian, as he did to everything in petticoats, and was probably much amused at this plain gauche woman's obvious infatuation for him. She was very susceptible, having had little experience of being courted, and her employer's " attentions " evidently went a little to her head, but her early puritan training and her tremendous belief in the inexorable law of consequences no doubt prevented her from going " too far." To return and face the irate Mrs. Chapman, and to live down whatever scandal there may have been, was, to one who believed as completely in accepting fully the results of her actions as did Marian, the only course possible. And she was eminently successful : no one except Chapman and his wife knew of whatever complications there may have been, and no stigma ever attached itself to Marian, whose reputation, until her liaison with G. H. Lewes, remained untarnished. Herbert Spencer at once on her return to London became a frequent visitor to the *Westminster* office, and since during this summer of 1851 Marian had met also two of her life-long women friends – Bessie Parkes, later Madame Belloc, and Barbara Smith, afterwards Madame Bodichon – these welcomed her arrival in town. Madame Belloc's description of her first visit to Rosehill is worth quoting, " Not Abelard in all his glory, not Spinoza in Holland, seemed to my young imagination more astonishing than this woman, herself not far removed from youth, who knew a bewildering number of modern languages and wrote articles in a first-class quarterly." Marian's new duties on the *Westminster* were very arduous indeed, often involving sixteen or eighteen hours work a day. She had to read all the articles sent in, to write the reviews and often the editorial notes ; she had all the proof correcting and actual editing of the paper besides. But she was very happy, for here at last was a work " important enough to demand the sacrifice of one's own soul," which Strauss so emphatically had not been.

Hers was now a very full and interesting life : she met, and not socially but on their own ground as fellow-workers, almost all the most brilliant men of the time : Carlyle will not write an essay on peerage, but recommends 'Browning the poet,' Froude writes on Job, Harriet Martineau writes on almost everything, whilst J. S. Mill comes out of his retreat to write an occasional article ; Mackay takes Marian for walks, Herbert Spencer sends her theatre tickets and takes her to the opera, and various lesser lights, W. R. Greg, Francis Newman and others, haunt the *Westminster* office. But of all these Herbert Spencer was from the first her most preferred friend ; handsome, thoughtful, a year her junior, his *Social Statics* had just been published and was having something of an ovation (" Lewes pronounces it the best book he has seen on the subject," writes Marian in September, not having yet met the " said Lewes "). Spencer, with all the qualities necessary for captivating Marian's heart, was a welcome relief after Chapman, who for all his good looks was not either as gentlemanly or as superbly English as Spencer, nor indeed could his intentions be called honourable. But although Spencer's intentions *were* honourable, he was never in love with Marian, though he delighted in her company, often flirting with

her in his rather ponderous way, and enjoying the
notoriety their friendship gave them. That was
absolutely the limit of his feeling. They would
spend long evenings together in Chapman's
garden, which went right down to the Thames in
those pre-Embankment days, and of which Chapman lent them the key. There they would talk
of evolution, of human happiness that was the
end and object of all philosophy ; and, writing
of these evenings later, Spencer confessed, " we
have been for some time past on intimate terms.
The greatness of her intellect conjoined with her
womanly qualities and manner, generally keep
me by her side most of the evening." Together
they went to concerts, and Marian made no secret
of her delight in his company : " My brightest
spot, next to my love of *old* friends, is the delici-
ously calm new friendship that Herbert Spencer
gives me. We see each other every day and have
a delightful *camaraderie* in everything. But for
him my life would be desolate enough." The
kindly Brays asked him to stay at Rosehill, and
Marian refuses to let him come until she is there
too. " He would prefer to wait for the pleasure
of a visit to you until I am with you, if you will
have him then." A little later, when people
began to talk about these evening visits to the
waterside garden, Marian explains to the Brays,
"We have agreed there is no reason why we should
not have as much of each other's society as we
like," and ostentatiously goes with him to the
opera. Marian and Chapman agreed to find a

wife for Spencer, but the young lady they produced (Marian herself) was, according to him,
too highly intellectual and had a " small brain
in a state of immense activity." However, he
presented her to his father, who, old Noncon-
formist minister though he was, took to her
greatly. Why Herbert Spencer never proposed
it is difficult to say, for he never married anybody
else, and must have realised how admirably she
would have suited him as a wife. He was the first
to see where her real talents lay, urging her to
write a novel, and it was he who introduced her
to Comte's Philosophy which they read together.
In his autobiography he gave a very entertaining
account of a meeting of authors convened by
Chapman at 142 Strand, " for the purpose of
hastening the removal of trade restrictions on the
commerce of literature," against the Bookselling
Association. Before the meeting Marian and
Spencer undertook to make a number of copies
of the resolutions, and Marian wrote hers far faster
than Herbert Spencer and astonished him by her
quickness. Dickens was in the chair, and the very
successful meeting did not end until twelve o'clock,
when Marian saluted Mr. Chapman with, " See
the conquering hero comes," on the piano, " for
not until then was the last magnate, excluding
Herbert Spencer, out of the house." It was very
unfortunate for George Eliot that Spencer did not
propose, for she would have written far more
simply, less defensively, if she could have " attained tradition " by marriage. It is never good

for anyone to feel an outcast, to be always on the defensive, justifying their lives to their fellow men, and George Eliot's implacable theory of retribution, her constant visiting of the sins of the children upon themselves, was in a large measure due to her unfortunate status in society. Had she married Spencer she would have had no such barriers set up against her : she would not have had to punish herself in the person of her heroines for what she had done, nor would she have needed the " senile, goody and prolix chorus " which she uses to emphasise every moral. She could have written for the sake of writing and not " to escape from mediocrity by giving a philosophical interest to common themes." After her death, Spencer wanted to publish a true account of their relations, in order to silence the newspapers, who were affirming that he had been one of her suitors, but he was dissuaded by Mr. Potter, who assured him that he would be " eternally damned " if he did. Whether Marian guessed that Spencer " did not mean business," or whether he himself explained his feelings, and if so how, is not known, but certainly by June the " affair " was all over, but without fracas, or even the shadow of a quarrel. They remained friends always – Spencer alone knew the secret of the author of *Scenes of Clerical Life*, and he was one of the last people to see Marian alive. Neither was her heart broken, only the shattering of what to her was love's young dream cannot but have wounded her sadly, and when she came to write

of a girl in love, but unloved, it was with exquisite
sympathy : Tina's affection for Captain Wybrow
and Gwendolen Harleth's love for Daniel Deronda
could not be more *felt*. But she had distractions
enough. Time and work are wonderful palliatives,
however great the pain. And Spencer had all
unknowingly appointed his successor. He had
introduced Marian as early as 1851 to George
Henry Lewes. Her first sight of him had been in
a shop, " a sort of miniature Mirabeau in appearance " she had called him, but it was Spencer's
bringing him to call on her in the Strand that was
their first real meeting.

CHAPTER V

Character and history of George Henry Lewes – his intimacy
with Marian Evans – they go together to Germany – her
family disown her.

GEORGE HENRY LEWES was even uglier than
Marian Evans. According to Douglas Jerrold,
he was " the ugliest man in London " and was so
unpleasing in appearance that children ran away
from him. A veritable scarecrow, tiny, with
quantities of hair all over his face and head,
bright eyes and drawn-in cheeks. Born in 1817,
the grandson of a once famous actor, he had been
miserably bullied at school, had then become a
clerk escaping from his office to travel abroad,
and had returned to England at the age of twenty.
On his return he had joined a philosophical club
in Red Lion Square, which had for secretary a
shortsighted Jew named Cohen, by profession a
journeyman watchmaker, who furnished George
Eliot with the model for Mordecai in *Daniel
Deronda*. Lewes was in turn preacher, medical
student (he abandoned that profession because
he could not bear to witness physical pain), actor
(he was popular in Shylock on account of his
appearance), and finally author. He wrote
several plays, three novels, and finally in 1845 a
Biographical History of Philosophy, which at the
time, being written in a popular style, had a
certain sale, but which Lord Acton dismissed as a
" vacant record of incoherent error." At the

time of his first meeting with George Eliot he was already something of a literary celebrity, and was above all an excellent conversationalist. Always witty and amusing, infallibly gay, he was everywhere welcome. In 1840 he had married Agnes Jervis, daughter of Swynfen Steven Jervis of Chatwell in Staffordshire, who was M.P. for Bridport and in whose family Lewes was acting as tutor. They came to live in London and Mrs. Lewes bore her husband a son. But the marriage was not a success as Agnes was lovely and extravagant, and Lewes was hard put to it to provide food, let alone luxuries, although he wrote as pot-boilers articles on every conceivable subject. To economise, the Leweses shared a house with Lewes' best friend, Thornton Hunt, the son of Leigh Hunt, whom Lewes assisted with the editorship of the *Leader*, and whose wife had been one of the " Rosehill " circle. Mrs. Lewes after bearing Hunt two sons whilst still living with Lewes, went off with him, and although she was persuaded to come back and Lewes forgave her, she went off again after a short while for a second and final time, leaving the three children, one of Lewes' and two of Hunt's, for Lewes to rear. Lewes could not get a divorce, partly because he was too poor, for in those days divorce was even more cumbersome and costly than it is now, and partly because his own mode of life can hardly be called moral.

" Legal obligation in marriage meant nothing to him or Hunt," Mrs. Lynn Linton, who knew him well, stated, and added, "to Lewes, life meant love and pleasure." But she admits that "where-ever he went there was a patch of intellectual sunshine in the room," and that he was extra-ordinarily attractive and always at his ease.

At first sight Marian was not impressed by him, although he was grateful to her for taking an article of his for the *Westminster*, "an agreeable article on 'Lady Novelists'" she graciously called it; but gradually she comes to admit that he has "quite won her liking in spite of herself."

She was having a very interesting time in London, meeting Florence Nightingale, making friends with George Combe, and reading *Villette* and *Esmond*, going to "the Chiswick flower-show, the French play, and the Lyceum" all in one week! She had made for herself a quite unique position : as Henry James truly said, "there is much talk to-day about things being ' open to women,' but George Eliot showed that there is nothing that is closed." Here was this spinster, unchaperoned, earning her living with-out any fuss, and meeting the greatest men of her generation as their equal : there was no question of condescension in their treatment of her. Mrs. Belloc says that she undoubtedly achieved a very great position in the London world quite inde-pendently of her novels, for in those years not a soul suspected her of a tinge of imaginative power. "My father," she adds, "was much attached to her, and whenever any special celebrity was invited to dinner, such as Thackeray or Grote, he was never content unless he secured Marian Evans," and on these occasions she was the only woman amongst " a group of remarkable men, politicians and authors."

Marian's " disappointment " over Spencer had hurt her more than she cared to admit, and she was glad enough to go for her holiday alone to Broadstairs, where she assured her friends she was " profiting body and mind from quiet walks and talks with nature," and later, after a visit from Mrs. Bray, who was clearly worried about her, she writes to her that she is " very well and ' plucky,' a word I propose to substitute for happy, as more truthful." She must have been a somewhat lamentable figure, collecting " lady's bedstraw " and " rest harrow " and other pretty things, but in October she went up to Edinburgh to stay with the Combes and really enjoyed herself : the Combes were well off and Marian loved " the order and elegance of everything about me " revelling at last for a few days in the " ladylike " luxuries she had sighed for as a child at Griff. She went on to stay with Harriet Martineau in the Lakes, thence to Rosehill for a happy ten days, and so back to London and work. And the very first day " after dinner came Herbert Spencer, and spent the evening," so evidently the break with him had been more a realisation on her part of his feelings towards her than any formal explanation.

Marian's brother-in-law, Dr. Edward Clarke, died this autumn and Marian's slender income was further reduced by her generosity to the widowed Chrissie. On her return to London, she arranged for her nephew to be sent to friends in Adelaide, and seriously thought of accompanying him. She was restless and discontented, although she confessed herself " in for loads of work next quarter." She spent the spring and summer of 1853 hard at work on the *Review* with occasional short visits to Rosehill. For August she went to St. Leonards and whilst she was there she made up her mind to leave 142 Strand and the Chapmans, and to find for herself lodgings on her own. She discovered what she wanted at 21 Cambridge Terrace, Hyde Park Square, and moved in October, telling Chapman in November that she wished to give up her work on the *Westminster*, although he persuaded her to carry on with it through the winter.

It was this move to 21 Cambridge Terrace which marks the beginning of Marian's liaison with George Henry Lewes. She had been seeing a lot of him during the summer, and had made up her mind that, although he could not obtain a divorce, the circumstances justified her becoming his mistress. During the winter of 1853 very few people knew of the situation. Chapman, one imagines, must have realised, although he had himself lost interest in Marian and his fickle heart had found another object of pursuit, which, incidentally, did not make life at 142 Strand any easier. Bessie Parkes was confided in, but not until just before the departure for Germany, and the

Brays probably guessed, from the new joyousness of her letters, that some change had occurred in her life. Lewes' position was by no means an enviable one : he had no private income, and was supporting, by hack journalism, and intellectual labours alone, his unfaithful wife, his three sons, and his mother. For nearly a year, although the intimacy of their friendship was obvious, no one seems to have suspected their relationship : Marian did as much as she could of Lewes' work in addition to her own : correcting proofs for the *Leader*, sending him off to the country when he appeared too frantically overworked, ministering to him and helping him all she could.

The new life benefited Marian greatly, and had a very favourable effect on her health. On her thirty-fourth birthday she wrote, " I begin this year more happily than I have done most years of my life. We may both find ourselves at the end of the year going faster to the hell of conscious moral and intellectual weakness, still there is a possibility, even a probability, the other way." She was, besides her *Westminster* work, busy with the translation of Feuerbach's *Essence of Christianity*, which appeared with her own name on the title page, the only time it appeared except in the privately printed *Brother and Sister* poems of 1869. Lewes meanwhile, had an anonymous play, *Joie fait Peur*, produced in London.

Marian went out a good deal that winter, seeing something of " a Mr. Huxley " and staying with the James Clarkes. But in April, Lewes became

really ill and Marian sent him off for a fortnight
to his friend Arthur Helps in Hampshire. On his
return his doctor still had grave views about him.
" His poor head, his only fortune," was not well
yet and Marian was very worried about him.
Finally she made up her mind. She realised that
they had become very necessary to one another.
Very well – this hole and corner life would not go
on. She would make a home for Lewes, would
unite herself to him openly, and comfort and
succour him all the days of her life. He really
was very ill, threatened with softening of the
brain from overwork and worry. So on July
20th she burnt her boats, gave up her rooms and
left with Lewes for Germany, with only a note to
the Brays : " Dear friends, all three, I have only
time to say good-bye, and God bless you. Poste
Restante, Weimar, for the next six weeks and
afterwards Berlin. Ever your loving and grateful
Marian."

It was a brave thing to do and a very hazardous
venture. Lewes was by no means of the type
that Darbys are made of, and there was a great
risk that he might quickly tire of the ponderous,
middle-aged, priggish and high-minded but
humourless woman who was giving up everything
for him. Marian was independent in means
" and of a worldly position hitherto high and ·
secure." No breath of scandal had ever attended
her : whatever her relations with Chapman, or
her infatuation for Spencer, the Victorian world
knew nothing of these. It is to be wondered why

Ee

she did not continue to live in London with Lewes
as her lover. But he was too ill, and she too
idealistic, for that. She thought her union
ethically justified – she had expressed her horror
once at Jane Eyre – " a diabolical law," she had
called it, " which chains a man body and soul to
a putrifying carcase " – and before she went to
the Continent she had satisfied her conscience by
going to see Mrs. Lewes, and asking her whether
there was any chance of her returning to her
husband. Mrs. Lewes said that under no circumstances would she return to Lewes, from
whom, however, she was accepting an annuity
(and continued to do so as long as he lived).
Lewes and Marian went to Weimar as Mr. Lewes
and Miss Evans and, apparently, only decided to
call themselves man and wife on the advice of
Mr. Helps, who met them at Ettersburg in
August 1854. Mrs. John Cash, Marian's old
pupil, emphatically and repeatedly declared that
George Eliot had told her more than once that
the legality of her marriage to Mr. Lewes was
merely a matter of geography – that while it
was illegal in England it was legal in Germany,
where a marriage service had actually been performed. But of this ceremony and this statement we have no proof. Marian had now, at
thirty-four, deliberately cast away her social
chances. In those days when divorce was severely
frowned on and the divorced forbidden the Court,
" living in sin " was beyond any and every pale.
No amount of extenuating circumstances could in

any way excuse it. She was completely cut off by her family, who regarded her conduct as a terrible disgrace and affront to them, and never wrote to her or spoke to her or had any communications with her except purely formal ones on business matters. After her marriage her brother relented so far as to write to her, and the dying Chrissie accepted her financial help, but she was cut off, root and branch, from the rest of the Evans family, some of whom, even after her death, continued to refuse to mention her name. Her women friends were more loyal : Harriet Martineau convened a private meeting of women to discuss her conduct, and although many were severe, there were some who were convinced that under the circumstances she had done right. Lord Acton describes the effect of her " lapse " as follows : " Ostensibly in accepting Lewes she was resigning a small group of friends, and an obscure position in literature. What she really sacrificed was liberty of speech, the foremost rank amongst the women of her time, and a tomb in Westminster Abbey." Certainly no marriage was ever happier than this strange alliance : Marian had found content at last and she and Lewes settled down to live a " conventional, respectable, mid-Victorian life." Their devotion to each other never wavered, and if it was Marian who gained most, for Lewes was not only a devoted husband, but nurse, secretary, literary and advertising agent and business manager as well, his work gained in depth and poise, and he himself was freed – after Marian became George Eliot – from the financial worries which had made his life a burden, whilst his three children were given a secure home and a very devoted mother.

CHAPTER VI

MARIAN and Lewes went first to Antwerp and then proceeded to Weimar. The Court there did not approve their relationship, but before the end of their visit, Lewes was invited to it and charmed that august assembly, and the two " sinners," who lived very quietly and studiously, in time met and made friends with several members of the ruling house, including Princess Marie, an " elegant, gentle-looking girl of seventeen." Lewes was collecting material for his *Life of Goethe* and he and Marian followed Werther's footprints, visiting the shrines sacred to the creator of *Faust*. Marian, pious disciple of Combe and Bray as she was, confessed herself bitterly disappointed by Schiller's skull and "amazed by the smallness of the intellectual region." They went to Ilmenau, and wrote their names in Goethe's " tiny wooden house " near one of the windows, where he had written " *Ueber allen Gipfeln ist Ruh.*" They made friends with Strauss and met Dr. Brabant again, and got to know Liszt well. He was conducting *Ernani* and *Lohengrin* (the latter bored them both stiff), and Marian delighted both in the musician and in his music, whilst Lewes

turned their acquaintanceship to good purpose by
writing an article about him. Liszt was a charming conversationalist and an amusing and delightful companion, from whom Marian, it appears,
drew Klesmer, the great music teacher in *Daniel
Deronda*. Liebig, too, they met, and Varnhagen
on Ense, and Rauch and Rubenstein, and
many others, spending in all, five very happy
months in Weimar. Their joint expenses, including wine and washing, were £2 6s. a week.
From Weimar they went to Berlin, which they
found far less attractive : the town was full of
soldiers and was bitterly cold. But even there
they made friends, and heard music and got
through an immense amount of work. Lewes
wrote his *Life of Goethe* and Marian translated
Spinoza's *Ethics* (this translation was finished but
was never published) and wrote articles for the
Westminster. She had already written on Carlyle's
Life of Stirling in 1852, now on her German trip
she wrote on women in France in 1854, and in
the first month of 1855 on Prussia and Prussian
policy, *Three Months in Weimar* and Vehse's *Court of
Austria*. Lessing's *Laocoön* delighted her, and
she infinitely prefered him to Balzac (it seems
strange to compare them), whilst *Nathan de Weise*
entirely altered her opinion of Jews. She had
hitherto disliked and despised them, objecting even
to "Dizzy" and to his novels, on racial grounds.
Thenceforward she was to admire them. The long
winter evenings were spent in reading Goethe and
Shakespeare ("all over again"), Marian reading

aloud in her low, lovely voice, and afterwards the
two drank coffee and ate pumpernickel together,
and these remained always some of her dearest
memories. But she found the Germans a little
heavy: " à propos of jokes, we noticed that during
the whole seven months of our stay in Germany,
we never heard one witticism, nor even one
felicitous idea or expression from a German."
It seems a pity that the Lewes' flight should have
been to Germany and not to France : the novel,
a very great critic has told us, must partake of the
nature of either poetry or science, and by her
Teutonisation of herself, Marian Evans bade
farewell for ever to Scott and Dumas and George
Sand, her childhood loves, and became, like so
many powerful minds of her generation, Ger-
manised. She forswore Romanticism entirely
and leaned heavily to the scientific in both her
novels and her life, threatening to swamp the
frail bark of her genius in the waves of analysis,
psychological clairvoyance, warning and example.
She tells, herself, how the idea of her first story
came to her : One evening in Berlin she found an
old exercise book, containing a description of
Staffordshire peasant life that she had written,
probably in 1846. This she read to Lewes, who
was very struck by it, although he " shared her
doubts as to her dramatic power." But knowing
her profound intelligence, he urged her to go on
with it and to take up novel writing. However,
at the time nothing came of it – for hard cash
was the immediate necessity, and, on their return

to England, on March 13th, 1855, there were a great number of problems to be faced.

Marian Evans – Mrs. Lewes as she now called herself – had written letters to her family and friends during her eight months' stay abroad : they had all remained unanswered. Even the Brays, broad-minded, sceptical, advanced though they were, maintained a grim silence. Marian was disappointed ; she had thought better of *them*, had hoped they at least would understand and con-done her conduct. She and Lewes halted at Dover at the Lord Warden. Seldom has that theatre of first nights harboured two people whose lives were at a more important turning-point. As Marian worked at Spinoza and tried to face the future she must have felt almost despairing. Somehow she and Lewes had to feed seven people on their earnings and on her tiny annuity. It was an overwhelming task, but at least socially they would be undisturbed and have no distractions ; of her friends, only Sarah Hennell, Bessie Parkes, Mary Cash and Mrs. Taylor continued to see her. After a fortnight in Dover, during which time Lewes visited his children at boarding school, Marian joined him in lodgings in Bayswater. They spent a week there and then decided to move out to the suburbs. First they went to East Sheen, where Marian wrote several articles for the *Leader* and sent the belles-lettres section to the *West-minster*. She took over the literary criticism of that paper, anonymously, and was very grateful for the work. She also wrote articles for Chapman

on Brougham's *Life and Letters* in June, and
in the evenings she read aloud the Iliad and the
Odyssey in Greek, and such lighter works as
Boswell and Sidney Smith. In June the *Life of
Goethe* was published, and was an immediate
success – it still is the standard English Life and
enjoys the distinction of being obtainable in the
Everyman two-shilling edition – and the financial
situation became a trifle easier. But they only
had one sitting-room, where perforce both must
write, and Marian, who was a bundle of nerves,
was nearly driven mad by the scratching of Lewes'
steel pen. Even after the success of *Goethe* she
doled out her sovereigns with the pangs of a miser,
and when, in August, Lewes took his boys to
Ramsgate for their holiday, Marian remained
in town and wrote her scathing article on
Mr. Cumming, a then fashionable Evangelical
preacher, whom she dealt with more than faith-
fully. This article it was which made Lewes
realise Marian's latent powers, and from that
time onwards he continued to urge her to try
her hand at fiction. But she was, at the moment,
too fully occupied : during the autumn she wrote
continuously for the *Leader*, reviewed for the
Westminster and wrote on Mary Woolstonecraft,
on Carlyle, Heine, and on Meredith's *Shaving of
Shagpat*. Lewes too was busy, manufacturing
articles and being facetious on *Lions and Lion
Hunters* and other kindred subjects. After a
brief holiday at Worthing for a " sea change,"
Marian and Lewes removed to 8 Park Shot,

Richmond, which was slightly more spacious than the East Sheen lodging-house. Life was complicated by Lewes' ill-health – there are constant entries about his " poor head " or face-ache, and he had to go down to his friend Arthur Helps in Hampshire more than once. Another annoyance was that, despite Marian's anonymity, her writings were constantly recognised. But on the favourable side of the balance was the recon-ciliation with the Brays, whom poverty – Mr. Bray lost nearly all his money about this time – brought to a more charitable frame of mind, and with Marian's half-sister Fanny, with whom she went to stay. Herbert Spencer, too, returned from abroad and came to dine. The difficult question of what to do with Lewes' sons was satisfactorily decided after a good deal of discussion ; Sarah. Hennell found a *pensionnat* at Hofwyl, near Berne, which was in every respect admirable, though very expensive. The two elder boys were taken there at once by Lewes, and the third joined them not long after. They all remained there for several years, during which time Lewes visited them regularly, whilst Marian tactfully kept away, although by degrees she began to write to them, and they to her. Whatever good or evil results Marian's union with Lewes may have had, it certainly brought salvation to Lewes' sons : no mother could have cared for them more, nor worked harder for them, and they as they grew older realised their obligations, and were sincerely grateful – the eldest, Charles, rising nobly to

Marian's defence when need came and championing her even against his own mother.

During the early spring, Marian wrote her articles on Riehl and Young, and in May they went down to Ilfracombe, where Lewes pottered about with glass jars collecting specimens, in preparation for his " seaside studies." They were both so hard up that they ascended the Tors only twice, " for a tax of 3*d*. a head was demanded on this luxury, and we could not afford a 6*d*. walk very frequently." On their return home, Marian wrote her essay on *Silly Novels by Lady Novelists*, and once more the belles-lettres for the *Westminster*. Her essays, in their attempt to be masculine, had out-Heroded Herod, for they were incredibly bitter and sarcastic – sometimes unjustly so – and Marian's later refusal to read criticisms of her own books may have its origin in her own harshness in the criticism of others. John Stuart Mill's treatment of Whewell's *Moral Philosophy* she had dubbed superficial, and " Byron was the most vulgar-minded genius that ever lived," whilst *Le Père Goriot* was a " hateful book." Her opinion of *Jane Eyre* has already been quoted.

Her essays are not in any way specially good. Neither her early Coventry efforts, privately published in 1919, which include from the *Diary of an Eccentric*, *How to Avoid Disappointment*, *The Wisdom of the Child*, *A Little Fable with a Great Moral* (rather a namby-pamby fairy-tale, *à la* Mrs. Scott Gatty) and *Hints on Snubbing*, nor her

Westminster Review essays, reprinted in book form, nor *Theophrastus Such* (a " collection of cumbrous and didactic essays which defy perusal ") merit, nor are likely to attain, immortality. In spite of her avowed affection for words, " Nathless, I love words," she had written to Miss Lewis ; " they are the quoits, the bows, the staves that furnish the gymnasium of the mind," she has no sense of form, no construction : there is in all her essays not one with a beginning, a middle and an end. Nor does she use words fluently : like Humpty Dumpty, she was apt to overwork them, but, unlike him, she did not pay them extra in consequence. She found " trying to make a certain idea thoroughly incarnate" a severe effort, and throughout her essays we feel the machinery at work ; as a witty Frenchman has said of her, " *elle s'écoute quand elle parle.*" *Silly Novels by Lady Novelists*, which dismisses almost all feminine literature (except Jane Austen) as " medical sweetmeat for Low Church young ladies," was for the moment her last essay : she wrote in her journal that she was " anxious to begin my fiction writing." At Tenby, Lewes had already begun to say " very positively " " you must try to write a story," and one morning, in a dreamy doze, Marian imagined herself writing a story entitled *The Sad Fortunes of the Reverend Amos Barton.* She told Lewes, who exclaimed in delight, " What a capital title," and from that time she had her story in mind. But it was not until September 22nd, after their return to Richmond, that she began to write. When she had started she told Lewes that she proposed to write a series of stories " drawn from my own observations of the clergy " and calling them *Scenes of Clerical Life*, opening with *Amos Barton*. Although he was still in doubt as to her dramatic powers, Lewes commended the idea, and said if the first story were good enough he would send it to Blackwood.

So here she was at last, this storm-tried matron of thirty-seven, now " dubiously known as Mrs. Lewes," settling down to her true vocation. For the next twenty years she was to produce " stately stories," and her first four novels, and her best, were to be " reeled off the camera obscura of Warwickshire." She was rather sad and introspective, and her return to the " dear old quaintnesses " of Arbury had in it more of the nature of a flight than anything else. Our most unfailing necessity is escape ; to create for our child's soul a garden where it may play whilst we are at our worldly affairs, getting and spending ; we must have our hiding-place where our hidden soul is invulnerable, where we can lift ourselves above all injury the world may do us. And Marian Evan's secret garden was the lost paradise of Griff ; for her, as for so many of us, her memory was her withdrawing-room, and there, where Augustine found the God he had fruitlessly pursued throughout creation, she found her true vocation, her consolation for the world's scorn, and found, too, the law of consequences, of

inevitable retribution, which she had seen work so
faultily on earth ; so " with old woes " she " new
wailed her dear times waste " and, "with the sugar
and spice of memory " extracted her honey from
the " wonderful cottage gardens which fill her
early pages with their colour and their odour."
She did not attempt to invent a story : no imagin-
ary events nor ideal passions for her. She ke; to
the facts. Her first story of Amos Barton was the
story of one John Gwyther, B.A., and his wife
Emma. He was rector of Chilvers Coton Church,
which Marian called Shepperton, and in Mrs.
Hackit she portrayed her own mother. Not the
people only, but the whole story, foreign countess,
and all, was true, and soon after publication,
written keys were passed round in Warwickshire
giving the real names of places and of people, side
by side with the names as disguised by the
author. Not one character nor incident was invented, and Milly's (*alias* Emma's) tomb became
a place of local pilgrimage. The habit of close
observation, coupled with a marvellous memory,
had enabled Marian to recall with remarkable
minuteness of detail the exact scenes and all the
particulars of a story which she did not invent, but
remembered, and whose chief characters were
friends of her father and mother. Even down to
Mr. Landor and Mr. Birdmain, each and all the
characters in *Amos Barton* were real people.
When Marian had written the first part she read
it to Lewes, who was delighted. He no longer
doubted her ability to carry on the plan – the

scene at Cross Farm convinced him that she could write good dialogue, and when she read him, a few days later, the death-bed scene, " we both cried over it, and then he came up to me and kissed me, saying, 'I think your pathos is better than your fun.' " So Marian went happily ahead and finished the story on November 5th. Lewes at once sent it off to Blackwood, with a covering letter explaining it was by a friend of his, " who desired my good offices with you," and confessing he had, before reading the MS., been doubtful of his friend's powers of writing fiction, but now that doubt was changed to very high admiration. He goes on to say he considers this story the best thing since the *Vicar of Wakefield*, and explains the series to Blackwood, assuring him that " the tone throughout will be sympathetic and not at all antagonistic." Blackwood's reply was conciliatory. He agreed to take the story for his *Magazine*, but although he wrote pleasantly he asked to see more before making " any decided proposition." He also criticised the story with great wisdom and insight : "Perhaps the author falls into the error of trying too much to explain the characters of his actors by description instead of allowing them to evolve the action of the story. The descriptions are very humorous and good." He had seen, what so many were only to perceive when *Romola* came to be written, the moth in George Eliot's rich attire, the moth of pedantry, a result of too much erudition encouraging " a natural tendency in her mind, which, as we have seen, was acquisitive rather than inventive." Lewes was, it seems, a trifle annoyed at the cool-tempered tone of Blackwood's letter : he could not bear that anyone should think less enthusiastically of his dear " Polly's " writings – as he called her – than he did himself, and he wrote again, claiming for *Amos* " that faculty which I find to be the rarest of all – viz., dramatic ventriloquism." Blackwood wrote back more warmly. He would start the series in January, and he was glad the author was a clergy-man – Lewes had alluded to " my clerical friend " – and when *Amos* appeared in the famous " *Maga* " it was given a front place, whilst the publisher added, " It is a long time since I read anything so fresh, so humorous, and so touching. The style is capital, conveying so much in so few words." Blackwood wanted one alteration ; that the names of all Milly's children should be left out, and Marian, although protesting, consented. " I have removed all names from the conclusion," she wrote to him, " except those of Patty and Dicky." She received fifty guineas for her story and the assurance that the rest of the series would be similarly published. The anonymity of the author completely mystified all readers. When Lewes read the stories to a party at Arthur Helps', they were certain the author was a Cantab. clergy-man, and the men at Blackwood's Club won-dered if the author were a fellow member.

On Christmas Day, 1856, Marian began *Mr. Gilfil's Love Story* and in February she sent the first two parts to Blackwood. It was during that

February, too, that she first used the *nom de plume* under which she was to become famous. While resolute in preserving her incognito, she sent Blackwood her prospective name as " a tub to throw to the whale in case of curious enquirers," and signed herself " Yours very truly, George Eliot." George, of course, in compliment to Lewes ; Eliot, because " it is a good mouth-filling, easily pronounced word." *Mr. Gilfil's Love Story* is, like *Amos*, a true story, and like Amos the characters are portraits. Even in her own lifetime George Eliot admitted this fact, and deplored it, promising that the mistake should not occur again and attributing it to the fact that " her hand was not well in." Mr. Gilfil himself was Bernard Gilpin Ebdell, rector, as Amos Barton *alias* John Gwyther was after him, of Chilvers Coton Church. The Cheverels are the Newdigates : Mr. Oldinport in *Amos* had already provided one picture of Robert Evans' employer ; his father was now portrayed as Sir Christopher Cheverel, and Arbury, which he had rebuilt in the Gothic style, and in whose library young Marian had been allowed to browse, is Cheverel Manor and is described minutely, room for room. Only Lady Cheverel comes out badly – George Eliot does not do her justice. Recently many of her letters have been published by Lady Newdegate-Newdigate, and reveal a most charming personality. She was very musical, and her Italian music master, Motta, was the original of Sarti. Once, when she was driving through a village, this Lady Newdigate

Fe

was attracted by the singing of a collier's little
daughter, Sally Shilton, whom she took home to
Arbury and whose voice she had most carefully
trained. This child was the original of Caterina,
but was never in love with Charles Parker (Captain Wybrow's original) as she was only eleven
when he married Miss Anstruther, whose name
George Eliot hardly disguised as Assher. Sally
did, however, marry Bernard Gilfil, but failed
to die romantically in childbirth, instead living
happily with her husband for twenty-two years.
As Sir Roger Newdigate died in 1806, George
Eliot's facts were chiefly acquired from gossip
heard in the servants' hall and housekeeper's
room, but considering they were gossip only, they
are remarkably complete and true – only Caterina's jealousy and death are invented. *Mr.
Gilfil* received an even greater welcome than
Amos had done, although this time George Eliot
set herself against any alterations and refused to
change anything – even Caterina's behaviour in
the gallery – to please her publisher. In March,
Marian and Lewes went off to the Scilly Islands,
carrying Mrs. Gaskell's *Life of Charlotte Brontë*, and
Sophocles, and Lewes' beetle-hunting apparatus.
They went on to Jersey, where she wrote the
epilogue to *Mr. Gilfil* and the first three parts of
Janet's Repentance. Meanwhile letters forwarded
by Blackwood continued to arrive from enthusiastic readers of *Amos* and *Mr. Gilfil*. Some
attributed the series to Bulwer, others, like Lord
Stanley, confessed their interested ignorance and

tried to pump Blackwood for the author's name. Most people seemed to prefer *Mr. Gilfil* to *Amos*, but Marian herself always preferred the former. In June they returned to Richmond where *Janet* was finished. Milby was Nuneaton, the Bull Hotel there, the Red Lion, and doubtless Marian's intimate knowledge of a bar interior came from listening to her father's accounts of local gossip and news he had heard there. Substantially, *Janet* is as true as the other two stories : the scurrilous Land Bill, the Dissenting minister preaching in church with the bishop's leave and being driven out of town by a mob headed by a drunken lawyer, all these are facts with which, as a girl, George Eliot was familiar. Dempster was a man named Buchanan ; Tryon a Mr. Jones; Prendergast, the Hon. and Reverend Mr. Stopford.

Blackwood was, according to the disappointed authoress, rather chilly about *Janet's Repentance*; he misunderstood the characters and seemed doubtful about some of the clerical details. Marian at once offered to close the series, but he would not hear of it, and *Janet* was published without alteration, but a fourth story that George Eliot had in mind, called *The Clerical Tutor*, never materialised owing to Blackwood's criticism. The . *Scenes* were republished in book form, Blackwood paying £210 for them, and their success waxed ever greater. Dickens at once guessed the author was a woman ; Mrs. Carlyle, whom the *Scenes* had comforted during a sleepless night, fancied

the author to be a married man with lots of
children and a dog; Froude confessed he could
not guess, whilst Thackeray was sure they were
not written by a woman. Tributes accumulated
on every side – as did cash. At last Marian and
Lewes were without financial anxiety; for the
first time, after paying for the children, the
housekeeping, Mrs. Lewes senior and junior,
there was a margin left. No wonder Marian
exulted, no wonder she wrote at the end of 1857
that " few women, I fear, have such reason as I
have to think the long, sad years of youth were
worth living for the sake of middle age. Our
prospects are very bright too." The *Life of
Goethe* was paying well and showed every sign
of continuing to do so ; Blackwood had accepted
Lewes' *Physiology of Common Life ; Seaside Studies*
and *Scenes of Clerical Life* were both out and
doing well. In October, Marian began her new
book, which she promised to Blackwood, against
whom she bore no grudge for his misinterpreta-
tion of *Janet*. It was to be a book full of " the
breath of cows and the scent of hay." In December, Blackwood called, and " it was evident to us
when he had only been in the room a few minutes
that he knew I was George Eliot." So the cat
was out of the bag as far as her publisher was
concerned, but it was not until the next spring
that John Blackwood, the brother, was told ;
Marian's secret was certainly loyally kept.

With the *Scenes*, Marian Lewes from comparative obscurity sprang to the front rank of living

authors. She has been acclaimed, and rightly, as one of the leaders of the naturalistic school ; George Moore and even Proust owe much to her, and the French writer has admitted his obligations. In her first four books, although the realisation of the moral side of life is never absent, it is present only as a sense of inevitability ; she accepts the natural consequences of each event without philosophy and without preaching. In these early days she can truthfully write that her function was " to be purely æsthetic, to paint and not to prove, and to glory in what is actually great and beautiful " ; and in a charming letter to Sarah Hennell in 1857 she says she feels a "greater disinclination for theories and arguments, in the presence of all this mystery and beauty and pain and ugliness that flood the world with conflicting emotions." She was content in the heyday of her life to let her memories flood over and into and out of her again, to become part of the great heritage which we call English literature.

CHAPTER VII

MARIAN wrote the first part of *Adam Bede* in the winter of 1857, and in the following March she and Lewes set off for Germany once more. This time they went to Munich, where the second part of *Adam Bede* was written. They went often to the opera, oftener still to the picture galleries, made friends, went excursions and had altogether a delightful time. George Eliot was never well in London ; once in the country, or, better still, across the channel, she recovered completely and immediately, and rarely suffered from so much as a headache. Whilst at Munich, Lewes went over to Hofwyl to see his children, and Marian during his absence received a visit from a Moldavian Jew, who was possessed by the idea of national redemption, and who is thought to have suggested Daniel Deronda. Lewes and Marian visited Vienna, Prague and Dresden, and so via Leipzig they came home. The last volume of *Adam Bede* was finished at Richmond by the beginning of November, Blackwood paying £800 for the copyright. Marian always alluded to *Adam Bede* as " My Aunt's Story," the germ of it having been Mrs. Samuel Evans' story of her visit to the condemned Mary Voce. But there are no portraits in *Adam Bede* as definite as those in the

Scenes, only "suggestions of experience wrought up into new combinations." Adam Bede himself was suggested by Marian's father ; Dinah Morris by her aunt, Mrs. Poyser by her mother and so on ; whilst the places are all the actual scenes of her childhood. But *Adam Bede* is more than the sum of its characters and its scenery ; it has the grandeur and the simplicity of the soil and of the people whose life is rooted in the soil. It is christened not with holy water but with the blessed earth, and through her absolutely naturalistic handling of terrene things, George Eliot obtains for her characters and for her novel the large utterances given only to those who regard earthly objects *sub specie æternitatis*. Hetty's lonely flight and Adam's vigil are but two instances of this power, on which the novel is as it were based. It is a cruel book and a sad one, for Marian "*avait durement experimenté de la vie*" and, though she bore life no grudge, she could not but describe it as she had found it. In *Adam Bede* she pays off many old scores : she, who had always been ugly and physically unattractive, punished Hetty Sorel for her beauty and her charm, and Hetty's flesh suffered for what Marian's had failed to enjoy. Poor Hetty was punished for another reason too ; Marian's whole creed, first as an Evangelical, then as a disciple of Mr. Bray's, later still as a Positivist, was that the wages of sin are paid C.O.D. ; her whole philosophy was a spiritual accepting of absolutely inevitable consequences. So, when in her own conduct of life she deliberately " broke all the pledges made and implied for her by her parentage and education," and found herself not persecuted, miserable, broken and punished, but richer, better, happier, and in every way more comfortable and more content, her remorse crucified her heroines – Hetty Sorel received what Marian believed to be her due. As, when a child, she had driven into her wooden doll's head the nails her wicked aunts should have endured, so now she made her books what her dolls had once been : the sublimation of her vision of retributive justice. This is true not of *Adam Bede* only, but of all her books and all her heroines ; because Marian had not scrupled to antagonise her family for the sake of the man she loved, Maggie Tulliver must suffer and die for doing so ; because Marian had attained her ideals, Dorothea Casaubon must be denied hers ; she herself became rich, Gwendoline Harleth she punished for her ambition towards riches; she gave up her traditions for love's sake, Fedalma must give up love for tradition's sake ; her love was satisfied, secure ; Romola's must be betrayed and cheated ; each wrong she believed she herself had committed she avenged in her novels ; each right she had failed to do she rewarded. Suffering had taught her sublimation ; Hetty and Maggie were her scapegoats, her sin eaters, her Polycrates' rings, nor were her novels past autobiographies only, nor flooding memories that could no longer be dammed up.

Adam Bede, published in three volumes by
Blackwood at the beginning of 1859 (" *that*
Bulwer's ' What will he do with it ? ' prevented it
coming out at Christmas as had been arranged "),
was immediately a success and rapidly became a
" best seller." The MS. was inscribed " To my
dear husband, George Henry Lewes " – an unfortunate piece of Victorian hypocrisy, which was
repeated in increasing doses on the front pages of
every one of George Eliot's books, even those
written at the Priory, North Bank, Regents Park,
only a few doors from where the real Mrs.
Lewes was living. Lewes was responsible for
two episodes in *Adam Bede* ; the fight between
Adam and Arthur, and Adam's marriage to
Dinah, neither of which can be artistically
justified, although when Sir Edward Lytton
mentioned the marriage and the dialect as the
two defects of *Adam Bede*, George Eliot stoutly
said : " I would rather have my teeth drawn than
give up either." Seven editions and sixteen
thousand copies were printed and sold during the
first year (1859), and Blackwood sent another
cheque for £800 and returned the copyright, at
the same time offering £2,000 for 4,000 copies of
her next novel. Within a couple of months
Adam Bede was quoted in the House of Commons, ·
and it was easily ' the book of the year,' being
translated into both German and French, and, of
course, as the *Scenes* before it, published in
Tauchnitz. The resemblance of the story to
Scott's *Heart of Midlothian* only serves to show the

differences between the two writers, for between
Jeanie and Dinah, Effie and Hetty, there are all
the years that separated the Marian Evans who
devoured *Waverley* and the George Eliot of 1858.

Between 1850 and 1860 was the flowering time
of Victorian genius ; *David Copperfield* opens, and
the *Mill on the Floss* closes, this fertile decade,
which produced *Vanity Fair, Pendennis, Alton Locke,
Esmond, The Shaving of Shagpat, Hypatia, Cranford,
North and South,* and *The Warden.* And of this
galaxy of talent, three books may be chosen as
representative of early nineteenth century England : *David Copperfield, Vanity Fair,* and *Adam
Bede.* They describe immensely different strata
of society, so different, indeed, that it is hard to
believe they existed contemporaneously, side by
side in the same country, but the great movement
upwards of the middle classes through the
acquiring of money, and the spectacular descent
of the upper through the losing of it, had not yet
begun, nor had the exodus from the country to
the town which was to have so terrific an effect on
conditions in England. By the time these three
novels had been written, all these changes had
come about, but it was with pre-war, pre-railroad,
and pre-reformed England that they dealt, and
of this England they are the truest pictures we
possess.

The financial success of *Adam Bede* made possible
the removal of the Leweses to a larger house,
all their own. In February 1859 they went to
Holly Lodge, Wandsworth, where for the first time

in her life George Eliot experienced 'servant troubles.' She was a real "home-maker," very feminine and orderly, but she found the delegation of authority to cook and housemaid, after having herself swept and cooked all her youth, very difficult, and she was for e er fussing about the house.

The anonymity of *Adam Bede* led to a curious annoyance for Marian. A crystal gazer or spirit rapper had given the name of " Liggins " as the author of *Adam Bede* at a séance, and this led to the discovery of one Liggins, a neighbour of George Eliot's in Warwickshire, by a Mr. Brackbridge, J.P. George Eliot remembered Liggins in her childhood – " a tall, black-coated, genteel young clergyman in embryo " – and upon this unobtrusive figure a delegation of Dissenting parsons now waited, and found him washing at the pump : he had, he admitted, written *Adam Bede*, and had given it freely to Blackwood, making nothing out of it. One of George Eliot's friends even wrote to her, asking her if she had read *Adam Bede*, and saying how funny it was of the *Westminster* to think the author a woman, when " here he is so well known." Largish sums of money were collected for him, and the rector of Kirby wrote to *The Times* stating categorically that " the author of *Adam Bede* was Mr. Joseph Liggins," whilst Blackwood received a mass of insulting letters accusing him of meanness towards the said Liggins. Marian wrote in vain to *The Times* contradicting the Reverend Mr. Anders, and even the Brays

continued to believe in Liggins. Only Barbara
Bodichon, writing from Africa, had recognised
Marian as the author of *Adam Bede*, merely from
reading reviews of the book. The Liggins myth
forced Marian to creep out of her incognito, and
soon all England knew who was the real George
Eliot, although no statement was ever made
to that effect. By November 1859 the Liggins
affair was concluded, but at once a new annoyance
appeared : Newly's advertised a book called
Adam Bede, Junior, and poor Lewes, who had devoted all his energies to the destruction of the first
impostor, now had to combat this new enemy.
Dickens came to the rescue and put an article in
Household Words on the subject, whereupon the
" rascally publisher was properly scarified."

Marian began to write again almost as soon as
she had put the last full stop to *Adam Bede*. In
April 1859 she wrote a short story, *The Lifted Veil*,
which purports to be imaginative and is rather a
dull failure. She was offered at this time £1,200
by an American publisher to write a story for the
New York Century, in twelve weekly parts, but declined, as it would take her from her novel. She
was already busy on the " The Tullivers, or Sister
Maggie," as she called her autobiography, which
finally was christened *The Mill on the Floss*. Sir
Leslie Stephen truly says: " In the *Scenes* she had
made use of the stories current in the early
domestic circle, in *Adam Bede* she had drawn a
portrait of that circle itself, and she now took
herself for a heroine, and the first two volumes

become virtually a spiritual autobiography." In her homeward journey she was come now to the innermost places, to where she was face to face with herself, and it was that self's face she now drew. It is her own Odyssey whose Ithaca is always behind and not before. It is George Eliot at her best, full of her " manifold but disinterested and impartially observant sympathy." It seems her childish pain had entered into its life of memory at last and had been changed into compassion. So, for two volumes, *The Mill on the Floss* is pure delight, the best we have of Marian's work. But the third volume is, alas, but " an enormous solution of continuity," as Swinburne said. George Eliot herself regretted the inadequate preparation of the tragedy, and the want of fullness in the third volume, due to her fondness for old memories. It was this fondness which entranced Proust. " Two pages of *The Mill on the Floss* can bring tears to my eyes," he wrote, and according to his own admission this work was one of the books which influenced him most. The *Mill* was finished on March 21st, 1860, and, on the 24th, Lewes and Marian left for Rome. The new masterpiece proved an even greater success than *Adam Bede*, the first edition of 6,000 copies being quickly exhausted. M. D'Albert translated it into French as he had translated *Adam Bede* and the *Scenes*, and even Queen Victoria admired it, which gave George Eliot great pleasure, " as always did any royal recognition." But there were dissentient voices even before Swinburne :

(who asserted that it owed a great deal to Mrs. Gaskell's *Moorland Cottage*). Ruskin called it " the most striking instance of the study of subcutaneous disease," and complained that the landscape was " of the Cockney school, by excursion train to Gravesend, with a return ticket from the City Road." Even Sir Leslie Stephen objects to Stephen Guest, the truth being that George Eliot could not portray men. There is not one *man* in all her writings, with the possible exception of Lydgate, and Stephen Guest is essentially female in character, giving the reader that same uncomfortable feeling that Peter Pan gives grown-ups. The *Mill* was dedicated to " my beloved husband."

CHAPTER VIII

Changes in George Eliot's surroundings – sense of incomplete-
ness without religion – *Romola* the defence and explanation
of George Eliot's creed.

WHILST *Adam Bede* and *The Mill on the Floss* were
being written, several changes had taken place in
George Eliot's domestic life. Her sister Chrissie
died of consumption, and George Eliot seems to
have helped to provide for her now orphaned
little girl. At the end of the Italian tour the
Leweses had planned, they took Charles Lee,
Lewes' eldest son, from Hofwyl, and brought
him home with them. The isolation with
which prejudice had surrounded Marian ever
since her "lapse" was rapidly breaking down,
and her success made many people condone her
"irregularity." She records of her third Christmas with Lewes that they ate their turkey in
happy "*solitude à deux.*" Their fourth Christmas
is spent with the Congreves, and later ones are
spent with Lewes' sons and their friends, an ever
widening circle. Public opinion began to excuse
her, and already she wrote to her husband's children nice, friendly, rather pompous letters, and
felt she could now consider having them under.
her roof. When a friend, Mrs. Peter Taylor, one
of the few really loyal ones, addressed a letter by
mistake to "Miss Evans," she received a severe, if
dignified rebuke. Marian took her irregular,
sub-rosaesque wifehood and motherhood very

seriously. She decided to leave Wandsworth :
there was little privacy in the house, which was
overlooked by a road, and there was no garden,
nor room enough for the newly acquired son.
But before the move, immediately on completion
of *The Mill on the Floss*, Marian and Lewes set off
on their long-projected Italian tour. Her first
journey abroad with Lewes had resulted in the
Scenes, her second visit to Germany produced
Adam Bede ; what would Italy do to her ? She
had great expectations, looking forward to " the
anticipation of the new elements it would bring
to my culture " and the " enlargement of my
general life." But her letters are singularly un-
emotional. Rome was a sad disappointment and
Mr. Lewes was as usual " enjoying bad health."
Yet, like the perfect husband he was, he never let
his sufferings interfere with any of his wife's plans,
nor did he write her letters, arrange her inter-
views, guard her privacy and maintain around her
the quiet leisure she needed, the less well for being
himself ailing – like a " headachy old woman," as
Marian describes him. In Florence, Marian
found that the world-famous statues of Michel-
angelo on the tombs (in the Medici Chapel) " remained to us as affected and exaggerated in the
original as in copies or casts." It was in Florence
too, that she first had the idea of writing an historical novel, and in Venice, Titian's " Annunciation " in the Scuola di San Rocco gave her the germ
idea of her *Spanish Gypsy*. In June the Leweses
came home again, and Marian wrote to Blackwood

that she would be very glad to see Bulwer's criticism of *The Mill on the Floss*, but particularly wished *not* to see any of the newspaper articles. The reviews of *Adam Bede* she had read, but they had decided her never again to read the reviews of her own books, and she explains to a friend, " I abstain, not from superciliousness, but on a calm consideration of the probable proportion of benefit on the one hand, and the waste of thought on the other." Mr. Lewes carefully cut out from any paper she read, or was about to read, all reviews, criticisms and, if possible, references to her works. This was not good for her, as it can never be good for anyone to wrap themselves in cotton wool against possible breakages. Already her false position had produced on her life a certain effect of sequestration, which was not favourable to social freedom nor to freedom of observation, and this isolation, whose temporary and admirable result was to throw her into herself, upon her own resources, and which resulted in her writings, " excited on the part of George Henry Lewes a protecting, fostering, precautionary attitude," on the assumption that they lived in abnormal conditions. Their actual physical isolation grew yearly less after *Adam Bede*, but by that time George Eliot had acquired, as it were, a habit of aloofness : she read confessedly very little contemporary literature, she saw very few people, and she withheld her work as far as possible from the effects of contemporary criticism. " It is," Sir Leslie Stephen says, " perhaps not altogether

GE

healthy for any human being to live in an atmosphere from which every unpleasant draught of chilling or bracing influence is so carefully excluded. Lewes performed the part of the censor who carefully prevents an autocrat from seeing that his flatterers are not the mouthpiece of the whole human race," and it is a lamentable pity that George Eliot did not go down into the arena and there compete with her peers : hers was a " take it or leave it " attitude, which, while it saved her work from the possible effects of outside influences, destroyed her own literary standards ; standards she had painfully acquired for herself, growing from a girlish admiration for Young and Hannah More to a real appreciation of *Villette* and *Dichtung und Wahrheit*.

It is difficult to over-estimate the importance of the Italian journey. She herself writes of it that it seemed " to divide one's life in two by the new ideas it suggests, and the new vein of interest it opens," and the change it wrought is from the woman who wrote, " My function is that of the æsthetic, not the doctrinal teacher," into her who said that every one of her poems " represented an idea which I care for strongly and wish to propagate as far as I can." The change was from reminiscence to creative imagination, and the consequent failure was one which " must always occur when an intellect which is purely acquisitive and distributive insists on doing work that is appropriate only to the imagination." Hitherto, she had been in the safe guidance of those " tired servants, her senses," now she resolved to abandon them for a Pegasus of her own rearing : her intellect-sodden imagination. The change was partly due to a return to her old vomit, positivism. Charles Bray had impregnated her with it ; on the *Westminster Review*, she had soaked in it, now at Wandsworth, where her next door neighbours were the Congreves, ardent disciples of Comte, she naturally fell back into her old ways of thinking, and not long after her Italian journey she exclaimed in a letter, "My gratitude increases for the illumination Comte has contributed to my life," and in later life she subscribed to the Positivist Society's funds, although she always " had her reservations," and although there were " details in Comte's work which did not satisfy her."

With the great success of her novels had come an overwhelming sense of duty ; duty to the public, to and for whom she was writing, and to whom she owed it to keep up her standard of excellence and to write nothing but what was helpful and inspiring ; duty to herself, to make known to all " the inexorable law of human souls, that we prepare ourselves for sudden deeds by the reiterated choice of good or evil which gradually determines character," duty as the inspiration of all conduct–in short, "that supremely hallowed motive which men call Duty." These considerations had not weighed very much with her until now ; she had written out of the fullness of her heart and memory, and if she had, as Sir

Edmund Gosse insists, seen " life as an organism, and, in her conte.mplation of the human beings she invents, been provided with a map," she did not in her early novels " abuse her psychological clairvoyance," nor dwell on it in hard and pedagogic manner. But after the Italian journey all is changed. With the exception of *Silas Marner*, the exquisite Benjamin of the Warwickshire idylls, every book or story or poem she writes has a doctrinal value which is its author's ultimate aim. She is writing no longer either to please others or herself, but to teach, to warn, to exhort, to exemplify. It is difficult even to guess how this change took place, how this deepening earnestness of gloom came about, for neither her letters nor her journals, as published by Mr. Cross, admit of the tiniest glimpse into her mind. Probably there were many reasons : some physical, some mental, mostly circumstantial. She had reached now the age known as " the change of life," and its reaction on her was probably to emphasise her girlish defects : lack of humour, intellectual aridity, and moral arrogance, too, of the sort that made Romola turn in loathing from her unfaithful husband, or Grandcourt despise Gwen Harleth. She had also exhausted her childhood's recollections ; had written herself out, and must allow that field to lie fallow. They say a tree blossoms most gloriously before it dies, and *Silas Marner* is the supreme and ultimate blossoming of the fragrant Griff tree. It is strange how long impressions took to incubate before George Eliot

hatched them into books : between Marian's
visit to the gypsies and her portrayal of Maggie
were over thirty years, between the riot at the
Bull and *Felix Holt* even longer, between the
sight of Titian's "Annunciation" and *The Spanish
Gypsy* were seven years, and between Coventry
and *Middlemarch* was nearly a lifetime. Only
Romola was written within two years of its inspiration, and there must have been some deep emotional undercurrent of disturbance to upset the
normally slow absorption of sensations by its
author. Possibly the realisation came to her in
Italy of the need for some spiritual and moral
guidance which, *Absente Deo*, would still be
above human questioning and to which all
individual whims would necessarily be subject.
She was, it must be remembered, the " first great
godless writer of English fiction," and in those far
off days the problem of finding a substitute for
religion was intense and acute, and one of George
Eliot's admirers has said of her that she was " the
emblem of a generation distracted between the
intense need of believing and the difficulty of
belief." Then still, since there was no God, man
was seeking to invent Him – the modern creed
that since He does not exist we do not need Him
and must manage without Him was not yet
evolved. George Eliot was continually sighing for
her lost deities, and confesses she would like to go
regularly into churches, since she enjoyed " the
delicious feeling of human fraternity " that she
found in every religious assembly. And the day

after entering in her journal, "Walked with George over Primrose Hill. We talked of Plato and Aristotle," she writes to Sarah Hennell, " One wants a temple besides the outside temple, a place where human beings do not ramble apart, but meet with a common impulse," and elsewhere states that " deism is the most incoherent of all systems, but to Christianity I feel no obje ion but its want of evidence." The impulse which drove her to write *Romola* was a religious one ; she wished to convince herself, and the world, of the efficacy of Duty and Tradition as substitutes for an eclipsed divinity, and she chose to work out her thesis in the person of a woman living in fifteenth-century Florence, at the heyday of the Renaissance, a time when the individual was faced with at least as many problems as in the nineteenth century.

Romola, apart from its historical aims, is a psychological confession of failure. George Eliot realised on that Italian journey, or just before, that religion or some substitute is essential to human society, that, to create either literature or life, it is necessary to be born not of blood nor of the will of the flesh, nor of the will of man, but of God. Yet it was not so much God she craved for as the coming together of the faithful. She had all her life been intensely lonely – even her life with Lewes was to a great extent a " *solitude à deux*," and being a woman of wide sympathies and large human interests, she hungered always for a society whose members, all working together for the common good, should be guided by their joyful and willing obedience to the inevitable laws of the universe. She sought in all her books that common formula which would unite Romola and her fellow citizens, or Dorothea Casaubon and the poor around her, and in Daniel Deronda she pictured her ideal human being. But her heroine, Romola, and her hero, Daniel Deronda, never became alive, much less human, for they are constructed without foundations, and are as ineffective as her pathetic creed, which postulated piety without God, renunciation without hope of immortality, virtue without the supernatural.

CHAPTER IX

Brother Jacob – Lewes' sons – *Silas Marner* – *Romola* – George
Eliot's health – Sunday evenings at the Priory – learning
Spanish – begins *Spanish Gypsy* – visit to Paris – Lewes be-
comes editor of *Fortnightly* – and literary adviser to *Pall Mall
Gazette* – George Eliot gives a party.

MARIAN and Lewes came back from Italy in
July 1860, and, having got rid of their Wandsworth
flat, they moved in September to 10 Harewood
Square, which they rented furnished for six
months. Later they went to Blandford Square,
where, however, they only remained until November 1863, when they migrated to the Priory,
which became their permanent home. House
moving, shopping and general upheavals were
very distasteful to George Eliot, who hated
leaving the green fields and comparative rusticity
of Wandsworth for London ; but Charles Lewes
had got an appointment in the Post Office and
was now living at home, so it was essential he
should be near his work. He was a clever and
very gifted boy, passionately fond of music ;
he and George Eliot played together a great deal,
and her letters are full of their mutual enjoyment
of the piano and of each other. Her relations
with her husband's three sons were perfect ; she
was devoted to them and they to her, and her
natural sensitiveness and fineness of feeling prevented the relationship foundering on the rocks
either of familiarity or jealous antagonism. For

all her clematis-like need of support and her
feminine clinging first to one man and then
another, she knew when and where to let well
alone, and the "intense happiness of her domestic
relationships was derived in a high degree " –
these are her own words – " from the perfect
freedom with which we follow and declare our
own impressions." Charles was naturally her
favourite – of his legitimacy there could be no
doubt, and he was, besides, far the ablest and
most gifted of the three. Yet she was careful not
to favouritise nor to make the other two boys
suffer in any way for their mother's sin ; Thornie
is her " grub knotted chick " and Bertie her
" cherub," and Thornton, aged fifteen, confided
to her how he gave the *Scenes of Clerical Life* to
" Dr. Müller's sister, a great friend of mine, with
whom I used two years ago to catch snails." He
left Hofwyl about this time and was placed in
" some more expensive position," being sent to a
college in Edinburgh, and coming to Marian
and his father for the holidays. This gave rise to
an absurd myth that George Eliot had a son by
John Chapman who was secretly educated in
Edinburgh !

On her return from Italy, George Eliot wrote a
story, *Brother Jacob*, which she first called " David
Faux, Confectioner," and which Lewes thought
worth printing. It is more of an essay than a
story, and its style is an unfortunate foreshadowing
of *Theophrastus Such*. She was already planning
her Italian novel and broke the news to Blackwood

in a letter dated August 28th, but after her
arrival in Harewood Square she began to write
Silas Marner. The idea of it had "thrust itself"
between her and the historical book she was
meditating, and she wrote it without the tears,
groans and diffidences with which she laboured
over her longer books. It is of its kind quite perfect
and is by far the best piece of *writing* she ever did
– no didactic passages mar it and the English is
unusually simple and direct. Mostly, her prose
gives the impression that "instead of finding the
right word she is accumulating more or less
approximations," but in *Silas Marner* there is an
air of spaciousness, like a fine landscape, so that
one wishes she could always have written on
subjects so suited to her hand, with such admirable
restraint. "The story," she told Blackwood,
"unfolded itself from the merest millet seed of
thought," the sight, as a child, of an old linen
weaver walking down the road with his sack on
his back. At first she had thought of writing it in
metrical form, but mercifully, "as her mind dwelt
on the subject, she became inclined to more
realistic treatment." Curiously enough, the
story is identical with that of the masterpiece
Jermola the Potter, of a Polish novelist, Krasweski;
but *Silas*, like the *Scenes*, is a Warwickshire tale,
although Raveloe is not on the map, and not one
of the characters can be even remotely identified.
It was the last rose of summer – *Romola* has already
a Michaelmas air. In March 1861, as soon as
Silas was finished and sent off, the Leweses left

for Florence, via France and the Corniche Road.
Marian delighted in seeing Avignon again – it
had impressed her on her first trip abroad with
the Brays – and loved the beauty of the Provençal
peasants. In Florence, although both were
unwell (poor Lewes was really very ill), they read
in the Magliabechian library, and " Lewes poked
about everywhere on my behalf," whilst they "for-
aged industriously in old streets and old books."
"Imagine," Sir Leslie Stephen suggests, "an intelligent Italian lady who had spent seven weeks at
the Charing Cross Hotel, walked diligently about
Leicester Square and the Strand, read steadily at
the British Museum and rummaged old book shops
in back streets ; how much knowledge would she
have acquired of the British costermonger ? "
And that was exactly what George Eliot did.
For thirty-four days she read Florentine history,
worrying desperately about the possible retarda-
tion of Easter and Savonarola's preaching in
Lent 1492, and then, from out of the books she had
read, she built up, " almost in Flaubert's manner
but without his magic," painfully and conscien-
tiously, her characters and her novel, dressing
up in language of her own what she had read in
Burlamachi or Villari. Before they left Italy,
Lewes and Marian were persuaded to join Mr.
T. Trollope in an expedition to Camaldoli and
La Verna, and his descriptions of their long mule
rides, and George Eliot's long speeches, are
charming and very vivid. They returned to
England in June and for the rest of the year

Marian busily continued her reading – she began
to write only on October 7th, but after a severe
struggle she gave it up and only began again in
January 1862. She was unbelievably industrious
and accurate, looking up costumes in the British
Museum, topography in old maps; and, indeed,
the list of books she read in preparation for
Romola gives the impression that she was about to
write a history of Florence. *Romola* was destined
for Blackwood, and George Eliot had no idea of
leaving her old publisher : but Lewes, mentioning
one day to George Smith, the publisher, that
" George Eliot had in hand an Italian novel,"
asked him to come to their house and to read what
she had written of it. She read most exquisitely,
and George Smith had always appreciated her
voice, but not until he had heard her read the
first chapters of *Romola* did he realise, to quote his
own words, " how deeply a woman's voice can
charm." " She had one of the softest and most
agreeable voices I have ever known and . . . the
next day I wrote to Lewes offering £10,000, a
sum without precedent at that time, for the book
for the *Cornhill*." The stipulations were that the
book was to be of a certain length and " to extend
through sixteen numbers of the magazine."
When the book was almost completed and its
publication about to begin, George Eliot told
Smith that she found she could not properly
divide the book into sixteen parts, and that she
must publish it in twelve. Smith could not agree
to this, as it would have made each instalment

too costly, so George Eliot accepted cheerfully
£7,500 instead of £10,000, rather than allow a
possible temporary artistic injury to be done to
her novel by its being first published in sixteen,
instead of twelve parts. Lewes seconded Smith
in his efforts to persuade George Eliot to keep
to the sixteen-part arrangement and to accept the
£10,000, for, as Smith writes rather caustically,
" Lewes was not so indifferent to money considerations as the woman of genius," but " George
Eliot was immovable and threw away £2,500 on
what many people would think a literary caprice,
but what she regarded as an act of loyalty to her
canons of art." After all these heroics, however,
she found she had miscalculated the length of
Romola, and eventually it appeared in fourteen
parts for which she received £7,000. It appeared
between July 1862 and August 1863. Without
Mr. Lewes' invaluable help it would never have
appeared : Marian's journal is one long wail
about suffering dreadful " palsy " or " headache
and malaise," and she describes how the writing
" ploughed into her," and when at last she had
come to the end of it she was completely exhausted. She hated having to work to time and
felt she was working under a " leaden weight,"
and, although this particular way of publishing
Romola had been urged upon her by Lewes, who
thought that it would be better for the general
public to read the book slowly instead of swallow-
ing it at a gulp, yet poor Lewes' bright ideas
were nearly always so unfortunate, and what

actually happened was that when people found it
was a serial, they either waited to read *Romola*
until it came out in book form, or just did not
bother to read it at all.   Mr. Smith found it a
bad bargain, financially, and George Eliot gave
him *Brother Jacob* for the *Cornhill* as a small
compensation.   *Romola* met with a varied recep-
tion.   According to George Eliot, " the immense
bigwigs " encouraged her and told her it was the
finest book they had read, but later opinion
inclined to agree with Henry James, who, although he admitted it was " on the whole "
decidedly the most important of her works, yet
complained that the setting was too large for the
picture and that it "smelt of the lamp," carrying
" to the maximum her indoor quality."   Swinburne repudiated it as a " laboured and over-
charged romance."   It is the first complete
exposition of George Eliot's creed, already
glimpsed at in the then unpublished *Brother
Jacob*.   Retribution, tradition : as regularly as
the ticking of a clock these two occur : from
" bare diagram to finished picture, they are the
constant theme and motive of her art."   *Romola*
is committed by birth, by choice, and by " respon-
sibility personally undertaken," to a certain way
of life and rule of action, from which there is no
possible dispensation nor escape.   As a picture of
Renaissance life it is singularly unsuccessful :
George Eliot has imposed on her 15th century
heroine a sense of moral obligation, a priggishness
of outlook and narrowness of mind which could

belong only to a Victorian prude, the workings of whose extremely involved mind are described in " an almost Germanic concatenation of clauses." Had *Romola* not pretended to be an historical romance, had she been " located " not in Florence but in 19th century Coventry, she would have lost nothing but her incongruity. This woman, appalled that her husband should have a mistress in the days when papal bastards ruled Italy, who regarded murder as incomprehensible, unatonaþe sin, is merely laughable. England has travelled far in insularity since Shakespeare portrayed the Veronese Juliet, and George Eliot was no "Englishman Italianate," her *Romola* is as confused and uneasy in her robes, as a débutante in a mediæval pageant. Nor could George Eliot complain she lacked models : *Hypatia* and the *Cloister and the Hearth*, both excellent historical novels, preceded *Romola*, as did *Esmond*. And, nearer Griff, there was Scott ; in denying Scott, George Eliot lost more than she knew.

Romola finished, and Lewes' *Animal Studies* also gone to press, he and Marian set off for a holiday to the Isle of Wight, where they delighted in cows and be-crinolined milkmaids. On their return to town they went to concerts and to the opera and generally relaxed after the strain of working to " time." Bertie came home from Hofwyl, too, so now there were three boys at home, all " bigger than their father." Thornton, however, soon left them. After failing in the Indian Civil Service examination, he was sent out to Empire-build in Natal. Bertie followed soon after, and, as Charles had meanwhile became engaged to a Miss Gertrude Hill (sister to Octavia Hill, of house-property management fame), when Lewes and Marian moved into the Priory in November they were once more able to enjoy their beloved tête-à-tête. George Eliot reserved her sympathy for her letters, characters and writings generally. She felt no enthusiasm for Causes, and although she confessed to being " rather ashamed to hear of anyone trying to be useful," she is content enough with her " dual solitude " and her constant holidays, nor did she ever feel moved to help in the great Victorian philanthropic movements. Perhaps it was better so : any woman can go slumming, but only one has written *Adam Bede*, and the artist, male or female, is happier devoting himself entirely to his one object.

George Eliot suffered a great deal from her stomach, and her letters are full of the misery of being dyspeptic. She had, all her life, constant headaches and a great deal of pain, but in the period which immediately followed *Romola* (after she had moved into the Priory and disposed satisfactorily of Lewes' children) she was stronger than at any time since her girlhood. One day she walked with George and Mr. Spencer to Hampstead and continued walking " for more than five hours," although almost the day before she had been complaining of her " terrible bad health," and she played tennis for hours on end almost to the end of her life. And at this time she actually admitted, " I am very well physically."

The Priory was a great success. It was decorated by one Owen Jones, who also took George Eliot's appearance in hand and attempted to array her " to match " her drawing-room, the result being all the most mediæval and Gothic-minded amongst her contemporaries could have wished. She and Lewes went up to the Highlands in the spring of 1864, and early in May they set off again for Italy with Mr. (later Sir Frederick) Burton, making a stay of seven weeks. Mr. Burton had been drawing George Eliot, and his picture of her now hangs in the National Portrait Gallery. She was portrayed several times ; M. Durade's portrait of her in oils at thirty still survives, and Mr. Samuel Lawrence, an American painter, made a drawing of her in chalks, front face, with her hair uncovered, in 1859. He later sold it to Blackwood, in the back parlour of whose shop it hung for a long time. Frederick Burton's study was an elaborate drawing in black and white chalk ; it was exhibited at the Academy of 1867, and after George Eliot's death Mr. Cross had it engraved by M. Paul Rayon. Mrs. Alma Tadema made a profile drawing in pencil in 1877 – the last portrait. George Eliot was once photographed : in 1850. She grew less plain as she grew older : her face gathered strength and lost some of its equine grimness. She looked, Morley said, " like a bishop," and Acton thought that " her aspect had greatness, but not beauty,

HE

so, too, her spirit had moral dignity but not saintly holiness." She had lovely eyes and a very attractive voice and a really welcoming, sympathic, maternal smile. To her, indeed, motherhood was, as Miss Haldane puts it, " a most vivid and vital impulse," and on her husband, her adopted children and the children in her books, she lavished a Madonna-like tenderness. Lewes was always " Paterculus " to her, or " dear little man and great author," or " the dear little Pater," and her care of his children has already been described. But real children never liked her, being frightened by her somewhat formidable manners and appearance.

Returned from Italy, Lewes and Marian settled down at the Priory. At first her friends, later an ever-widening circle of admirers, of literary contemporaries, of young authors and visitors from overseas, came to visit her on Sunday evenings, and at these simple gatherings Lewes was host and hostess in one, for George Eliot always found talking to more than one person at a time very bewildering and insisted on keeping the conversation upon earnest and deep topics : eternal verities took the place with her of the usual banalities of social intercourse. Gradually these Sunday evenings developed into a regular *Salon*, where crowds of breathless worshippers waited upon the " wise, witty, and tender sayings " which fell from her lips. But always Lewes' gaiety, charm and Bohemian naïveté kept the assemblies from becoming the merely intolerably

boring and artificial conglomerations of people
they might so easily have been.

In the autumn of 1864, George Eliot's thoughts
turned again to the writing of verse. She had
been reading Spanish history, and had been so
much absorbed by it that she began to learn
Spanish and mastered easily " the easiest of all
the Romance languages," as she called it. She
always found learning easy – womanlike, she enjoyed lessons for their own sake, and would have
loved examinations had she lived some fifty years
later. " I feel it is so much easier to learn anything," she wrote, " than to feel I have anything
worth teaching." She began now to write blank
verse, having in mind to write a drama whose
subject would have a background in Spanish
history. At first the work went well : " G."
praised and encouraged, and the first act was
completed by October 5th. But as the winter
came, and the fogs and cold, and George Eliot's
health declined, to be restored only when spring
returned and the sun (" the soul's calm sunshine
in me is half made up of outer sunshine "), the
drama went less well. The second and third acts
were written, and Lewes, as usual, was all admiration, but Marian felt something was wrong.
In January 1865 they went for ten days to Paris,
but of this visit Marian has little to say. Con-
trary to her usual Baedeker minuteness of description, she has no words for the streets, the
people or the galleries. Only Comte's dwelling-
place affected her ; Paris was definitely not her

milieu. The levity, the mocking wit, the gay satire of the great city and of its inhabitants jarred on her serious, sedate nature ; " light and easily broken ties," which she so abominated, were the rule there rather than the exception, and she infinitely preferred the " large serious views which are a special product of German culture." Nor had the Parisians any use for the plain, dowdy, provincial lady who gave herself solemn airs and carried around a " p'tit bout d'homme," who waited on her like a comic knight errant. On their return the Spanish drama still hung fire, and Lewes' acceptance of the editorship of the *Fortnightly*, which " was to be partly on the plan of the *Revue des deux Mondes*," and of the post of Literary Adviser to the *Pall Mall Gazette* at £600 a year, meant a lot of extra work for them both. The *Pall Mall* was owned by the publisher of *Romola*, and Marian was much interested by these two attempts to raise the standard of periodical journalism. It was in the *Fortnightly* that signed reviews, which have become so universal, first appeared. Marian sent articles to the *Pall Mall* on the "Logic of Servants" and on "Futile Lying," and to the *Fortnightly* she sent a severe criticism of Lecky's *History of Rationalism*, shortly after having expressed the opinion, to Sarah Hennell, that critics were people, " obliged to say striking things, who did not engage a very high grade of conscience or ability." In her position as wife of the *Fortnightly's* editor, she and Lewes decided to give a party ; music, food, charades,

all were provided, but it proved a " mull." Only
twelve intimates appeared ; the weather or illness provided some with excuses ; others simply
did not turn up. After twelve years of living
quietly, of hiding her head, the public opinion oı
middle-class London society (and of the so called
" intelligentsia " at that) did not consider
Marian's position secure or established enough to
warrant their accepting her hospitality. Quiet
Sundays at home, perhaps, but a grand party, as
though their situation were normal, orthodox,
traditional – certainly not. Marian seems to
have felt the intended slight, for two days later
she writes from her bed that she is " ill and very
miserable – George has taken my drama away
from me."

CHAPTER X

Felix Holt – The Spanish Gypsy – George Eliot's verse – *Middle-march – Daniel Deronda.*

By March, Marian had begun to recover from her
usual wintry ill-health and fretfulness and from
the failure of her party. She began a novel,
which was finished in little over a year and was
called *Felix Holt, the Radical.* In it she returned to
England but not to Griff. The gates of Paradise
were closed for ever now, and this novel deals
with Coventry, not Shepperton, and with town life
and folk. Over the complicated legal questions
she consulted Frederick Harrison, who corrected
her law and generally helped with the construction of the tale, but with her usual thoroughness
she herself consulted Sugden and *The Times*
of 1832–3. Lewes asked £5,000 for *Felix Holt,*
which Smith declined to pay, but Blackwood
gave the sum asked and Marian returned to her
first publisher, never to leave him again, without,
however, ceasing to remain friends with Smith,
as she had remained friends with Blackwood even
while Smith was publishing *Romola.* *Felix Holt*
was ready on May 31st, 1866, and published in the
autumn of the same year. It is a curious story,
full of lost heiresses and illegitimate sons, rascally
lawyers and noble workmen and it seems an attempt both to clear her mind politically and to
preach her politics, just as *Romola* was a clarification

of her views on religion and matrimony no less
than an attempt to propagate these views.
There is something of herself in Esther Lyon – of
the self that hungered for the " signs and luxuries
of ladyhood " and held herself aloof from her
companions – of the self, too, that argued with
young Charles Hennell, and listened to the ser-
mons of old Dr. Franklin. It is the worst of her
novels. The hero is as completely straw-stuffed
a Radical as ever were the dummies British tom-
mies bayoneted in Hyde Park. He has milk and
water – the milk of human kindness and plenty
of cold water to pour on all who disagree with
him – in his veins, and poor Esther must have
suffered greatly from being bedfellow to such a
prig. Mrs. Transome alone, the bitter, pathetic
old woman, whose " knowledge and accomplish-
ments had become as valueless as old-fashioned
stucco ornaments, of which the substance is no
longer worth anything, while the form is no longer
to the taste of any living mortal " is alive, and in
her also is something of George Eliot – of the
George Eliot who complains of " the years of
retrieval that keep shrinking," and who is constantly " in a deep depression, feeling powerless,"
or " going doggedly to work, seeing what determ-
ination can do in the face of despair." No writer
has ever got less joy out of her work : George
Eliot never really liked writing any of her books
after *Adam Bede*, with the one possible exception
of *Silas Marner*. The effort of keeping up her self-
imposed standard led to a constant falling " into

a state of so much wretchedness in attempting to concentrate my thoughts on the construction of my novel." Hers was triumph without song, feast without shouting, and *Felix Holt* is, after *Romola*, the novel in which, not only can the machinery of the author's mind be most clearly seen, but also in which the friction is greatest and most perceptible. As a political novel, *Felix Holt* is a bad third to *Alton Locke* and *Sybil*.

George Eliot was inevitably conservative, and, not content with preaching her die-hardism through the mouth of Felix – a Toryism not political but psychological and fundamental – she proceeded to publish in *Macmillan's Magazine* an address " to working men " (purporting to be by Felix Holt) which is singularly inept. It appeared in 1868 and was the last contribution George Eliot made to periodical literature.

After finishing *Felix Holt*, Lewes and Marian went abroad, as usual : this time to Holland, Germany, Belgium and so home. In Amsterdam they attended Jewish worship in a synagogue ; and the chanting and swaying about of the bodies, 'almost a wriggling,' made a profound effect on Marian, so great indeed that it led her ultimately to write in *Daniel Deronda* of the " faint symbolism of a religion of sublime, far off memories." Gradually Judaism took an ever greater hold on her imagination, until, although she never outwardly adhered to the Jewish faith, she may be said to have accepted its ethics and ideals. Back in England she took up the idea again of her drama and read Spanish subjects in preparation. She had re-read it and finding it impossible to abandon she wrote confiding her intention to Frederick Harrison. In December she and Lewes set off for Spain, where they remained, travelling about diligently and working hard no less than enjoying themselves, until March. She continued to work at her drama until July, when she and Lewes went a tour in North Germany, taking *The Spanish Gypsy* with them, and after they came home in September she still laboured on at it until the end of April 1868. She had spent endless time reading such remote books as *Averoës et l'averoïsme*, the Iliad, Lubbock's *Prehistoric Ages*, and Victor Hugo's poems. But on April 29th, *The Spanish Gypsy* was at last finished, and this " mass of positivism " was published almost immediately. The plot, which George Eliot conceives to be grander than that of *Iphigenia*, is, according to Sir Leslie Stephen, an absurd dilemma. " We do not see why the daughter is bound to act like a lunatic. We cannot perceive that her motives are reasonable and intelligible, and her doctrine is that our principles are to be determined by the physical part of our ancestry." The verse is laboured and heavy, a badly made fake of real poetry, and the drama suffers from Lewes' physical and scientific views on life, no less than from the course of Dr. Congreve's lectures on Positivism which George Eliot attended assiduously during the winter of 1867–8. With such pre-natal influences attending it, what is remarkable is that *The Spanish Gypsy*

is not worse than it is. George Eliot herself seems
to have had no conception of her limitations and
never to have realised her inability to write verse,
confident in Professor Sylvester's " laws for verse
making," which she found so useful [when she
told Tennyson this he exclaimed, " I can't understand that "], and in Lewes' " unprecedented
delight " and in his " state of beatitude about
the poem." Sir Edmund Gosse has an interesting
theory that George Eliot took to verse, and devoted
nearly a quarter of her literary career to it, because she realised " what was her chief want as a
writer of imaginative prose." He considers that
" she was consciously in want of some element
essential for her success " and that she hoped to
obtain it by hammering herself into poetry by
dint of sheer labour and will power. She was
now forty-four, and she had spent already three
years writing her Comtist tragedy and was to
produce quite a large body of various verse, in
her search for the " chanting faculty in prose,"
which the greatest writers possess and which she
so singularly is without. It is an interesting
theory and one likely to be true, for George Eliot
was an extraordinarily intelligent woman, and
even the absurd devotion and flattery, laid on
with a trowel by her devoted husband and fol-
lowers, could not quite stupefy her excellent
critical faculties. She realised that to leave Griff
was to leave hold of her surest staff, yet knew she
could not return thither, and she floundered in
many deep waters before she found her feet again.

Stephen's criticism of her verse is masterly : he
calls the lyrics in *The Spanish Gypsy* " palpable
if clever imitations of the genuine thing." Of her
other poems, all written about this time, the
" Legend of Jubal " is perhaps the best. " How
Mira Loved the King," " Agatha," " A Cottage
Breakfast Party," are others of her longer poems,
the latter described by Gosse as reconstructing all
Tennyson's faults, " on the plan of the Chinese
tailor who carefully imitates the rents in the English coat he is to copy." " Orion " is stately in
the manner of Marvell, but in all her poems, one
feels, her verse was to her a fetter, not an inspiration. Miss Haldane would defend her poetry
because it " raised the thoughts of men and
women to higher things," but that object, however
admirable, was never the purpose and rarely the
effect of poetry. Her most famous poem, " O
may I join the Choir Invisible," which was used
as a Positivist hymn, and is a complete expression
of her matured religious views, is rather pathetic,
for it is very doubtful if she was ever a " cup of
strength in some great agony," being more often
quoted as an argument in adultery. (In the
'seventies and 'eighties of last century, apparently,
to discard marital obligations was commonly
called " living à la George Eliot.") In 1869 she
had privately printed five sonnets, *Brother and
Sister*, in which she returns to the Red Deeps
and the brown canal at Arbury, and which are
the least *voulu* of her poems. But the simpler
style in which she wrote them was short-lived ;

soon after their appearance, she begins a poem,
" I have a friend, a vegetarian seer, by name
Elias Baptist Butterworth." Her collected verse
was published in one volume in 1874, and George
Eliot tells Blackwood that " the form of volume
I have in mind is a delightful duodecimo edition
of Keats' poems (without the " Endymion ") published during his life : just the volume to slip in
the pocket. Mine will be the least bit thicker."
She had already chosen the title, *The Spanish
Gypsy*, because she felt her cousinship with the
elder dramatists. (Middleton's *Spanish Gypsie* was
produced in 1621.) But after the slim Keatsian
volume, George Eliot forswore verse : she seems
at last to have realised that she could " never hope,
with all her intellect, to catch the unconsidered
music which God lavishes on the idle linnet and
frivolous chaffinch."

As soon as *The Spanish Gypsy* was in print (the
MS. was dedicated to " my dear – every day
dearer – husband "), Lewes and Marian left London for Germany, where she made Baden Baden
her headquarters. Home again, she visited
Sheffield and Matiock and the country around
her old home, and it was on this visit that she saw
a new hospital in Leeds which was to influence
her next novel considerably, being the original of
Lydgate's ideal. In March 1869 she and Lewes
went abroad again, to Italy this time, and it was
in Rome that she met her future husband, Mr.
John Cross. Herbert Spencer had introduced
Lewes to Cross's parents, and Lewes had brought

them to George Eliot, with whom they had made
great friends. Mrs. Cross made no objection to her
daughters frequenting the great authoress, and
these young people, almost the only ones she
knew (her Charles's Gertrude and Mrs. Congreve's
Emily being practically the only others), were a
great delight to Marian. Mr. Cross was a
banker in New York, some twenty-five years her
junior. He, at once, on sight of her, joined in his
family's devotion to her, and in the following
August the two families met again at Weybridge,
the Crosses' home. There the friendship was
cemented by the sudden death of John Cross's
married sister, in childbirth, but a month after
she had set *The Spanish Gypsy* lyrics to music.
Marian had sorrow at this time too, for Thornton
Lewes came home from Natal to die. He was
only twenty-five, but sadly wasted by suffering
from a " long standing spinal injury." He lin-
gered from May to October, and George Eliot
nursed him devotedly, even sending for his real
mother and, when she came, keeping carefully out
of the way. During that bitter waiting upon
death Marian wrote a large part of *Middlemarch*.
She had projected it in January 1869 but did not
begin to write " Miss Brooke " till August 1870.
This was the longest of her novels, so lengthy
indeed that it alarmed Blackwood, but George
Eliot was adamant, and the four-volume novel
appeared in eight parts, the first in December
1871, the last in December 1872. It is the epic of
English middle-class, mid-Victorian, Midland life,

written by a middle-aged woman. She made over £8,000 on it, and by Christmas 1879 she had sold thirty-three thousand copies, the first few editions at two guineas, the later ones at one, and it was received with greater enthusiasm than any of her former books, *Adam Bede* not excepted. Her admirers were delighted at her return to fiction, and though this new serious long book was not " starred with flashes of delicious humour like the lemon yellow pansies and potentilla on a dark Welsh moor " as *Adam Bede* and the *Mill* had been, yet their delight was not diminished. To get her medical details right, George Eliot had soaked herself in medical literature, had gone with her husband to Berlin, where he was working at psychology at the Charité Hospital, and had, whilst staying with the Pattisons at Oxford, seen a brain dissected. Her legal knowledge she also "rubbed up" with such success that "the lawyers expressed their astonishment at the ingenuity and correctness of the law " ; whilst Sir James Paget himself " commended the medical details and the insight into medical life." But she had profited by her mistakes in *Romola* and *Felix Holt*, and there is no burdensome accuracy, no boring pedantry, no undue emphasis on undigested facts, in *Middlemarch*. It is a superb novel, one of the greatest that the 19th century produced, and, as an unforgettable picture of the small town in Victorian England, it is unique. What Sinclair Lewis has done for America in *Babbitt* and *Elmer Gantry*, George Eliot has done for her England in *Middlemarch*,

but how far subtler, how more supremely
intuitive, is her handling of the characters.
Beside Bulstrode, Elmer is an overdressed carica-
ture, and even Martin Arrowsmith in his youth
has not the glorious optimism and ambition that
beset young Lydgate.[1] The influence of *Middlemarch* can be seen in many places : besides Proust,
Hardy felt it, and Flaubert and Mr. George
Moore. It is the sublimation, the idealisation of
George Eliot's Coventry days, her experiences
there are lifted up and transfigured. In her
earlier Warwickshire books the transformation is
not complete ; she reproduced her characters
from living people without being aware of the
degree of likeness ; now that she had transfigured
herself, through work, through suffering, through
living, she was able to lift her characters up to the
level she herself had attained. Caleb Garth is a
final tribute to her father ; Dorothea, a final
crucifixion of herself ; Celia a charming remem-
brance of Chrissie ; Casaubon part Mark Pattison,
part Dr. Brabant, part herself (she pointed to her
own heart when asked where she found him), yet
he is wholly himself. The conflict between
Dorothea and Casaubon is best understood by the
conflict between the author's two natures – that of
the dry scholar, accumulating useless knowledge,
and that of the aspiring woman, prisoned awhile,
by Strauss, by housekeeping, by disappointments

[1] With the present day undergraduates at Princeton, George
Eliot "goes bigger" than either Jane Austen or the Brontës ; *Silas
Marner* is disliked, but *Adam Bede*, *The Mill* and above all, *Middle-
march* " decidedly score."

in love, but blossoming into true happiness when
she meets Lewes. Dorothea must give up the
legacy left her by her husband to marry Will, as
Marian must give up all her old associations,
faiths, moralities and friends to live with Lewes ;
and it is by no mere chance that Will Ladislaw is
drawn like Lewes : poverty-stricken, hirsute, ugly,
mercurial, a jack-in-the-box, a jack of all trades
and master of none. Marian's love was so great
that she saw Lewes as he was and loved him
still : that second-rate little whipper-snapper, that
failure, was the one man she and her Dorothea
loved, respected, obeyed.

After *Middlemarch* Marian received something
of an apotheosis. The Priory " at homes "
were more crowded than ever ; Tennyson and
Turgieniev, Meredith and Trollope, Rossetti and
Acton, Harrison and Burne-Jones, crowded about
her. A Mr. Main compiled an anthology of her
" wise, witty and tender sayings " ; a Mrs. Stuart
called her " Madonna," or " mother," and
received in exchange " the sweet name of daughter," whilst loading her continually with every
imaginable sort of present from woollen scarves
and carved bookcases to slippers and eggs, and
finally was buried next her at Highgate. The
usual post-book-completion voyage was taken
after *Middlemarch* – this time to Homburg, where,
amongst the crowd of gamblers, Marian saw a
young girl who suggested to her the opening
scene of her next book. Already in June 1874
she was " brewing her future big book," and the

issue of it began on February 1st, 1876. It was
finished in June 1876 and was published in book
form, at two guineas per volume, after the last
issue had appeared in September of the same year.
As *Middlemarch* had been three stories concur-
rently, so *Daniel Deronda* is the history of two
wholly different lives. Gwendolen Harleth is
magnificently drawn – the greatest woman George
Eliot created, but her husband is a feeble sort of
villain whose wickedness is very far removed from
our present morality. A modern Daniel would
tell Gwendolen that there was no earthly reason
why Grandcourt *should* marry his mistress or give
her the family jewels, that he was an attractive
fellow but pompous and conceited, and that the
sooner she bore him an heir the better. As for
Daniel himself, he is, as Stevenson so expressively
remarked, " a melancholy puppy and humbug,
a prince of prigs, a literary abomination and
desolation in the way of manhood, a type which
is enough to make man forswear the love of
women, if that is how it is to be gained." His
appearance was taken from the head of Christ
in Titian's "Tribute Money," and his death is not
only reminiscent of George Eliot's grandfather's
drowning, but also of a story by Paul Heyse, published in 1858, in which a Neapolitan fisherman's
momentary hesitation in rescuing his drowning
friend causes his death, whilst his friendship with
Meyrick was based on the companionship of two
men whom George Eliot had remarked upon in
the Balliol College common-room. The Jewish
IE

part of the story is as unreal as Romola's Florence, but, read as a foreshadowing of the modern Zionist movement, it is not uninteresting. *Daniel Deronda* sold as well or better than *Middlemarch*, but the " inner circle " of Marian's admirers were beginning to ask one another uneasily whether " her method was not now too calculated, her efforts too plainly premeditated." Some there were, like Henry James, who remained a very "Deronda of the Derondists, for my own wanton joy ; which amounts to saying that I found the figured, coloured tapestry always vivid enough to brave no matter what complications of stitch." But others there were also – Swinburne amongst them – who thought that *Daniel Deronda* showed, as did *The Spanish Gypsy*, "how much further and more steadily and more hopelessly and more irretrievably and more intolerably wrong it is possible for mere intellect to go than it can be for mere genius." But then it was Swinburne who " discovered " Charlotte Brontë to be so much greater than George Eliot ; and to-day we might be inclined to reverse the verdict, to regard George Eliot, " the type of intelligence vivified and coloured by a vein of genius," as preferable to Charlotte Brontë's " type of genius directed and moulded by a type of intelligence," for the Brontës are become a trifle outworn, whilst *Middlemarch* and even *Daniel Deronda* – for all its absurdities – have been unduly neglected. *Daniel Deronda* was George Eliot's last novel. In a letter to Dr. Albutt, as early as 1873, she had said " some time

or other, if death does not come to silence one,
there ought to be a deliberate abstinence from
writing, a self-judgment which decides that one
has no more to say " ; and, it seems, now this
time had come.

CHAPTER XI

DURING the years 1870–6, whilst George ᴸliot
was writing *Middlemarch* and *Daniel Deronda*,
Bertie, Lewes' youngest boy, died in Africa,
leaving a wife and two children behind him.
They came home to England and appear to have
been supported by Lewes and Marian. George
Lewes' old mother died, and Gertrude Lewes
presented Lewes and Marian with three pretty
grandchildren.

George Eliot's books were translated into Dutch
and Hungarian, and the two new novels and *The
Spanish Gypsy* were translated into German. In
December 1876 she and Lewes bought the
Heights, Witley, a largish house near the Crosses
and Tennyson, with eight acres of ground. Owing
to the " dreadful state of the money market "
this house cost them £3,000 less than was asked.

On January 1st, 1877, Marian notes in her
journal that " all is happiness, perfect love, and
undiminished intellectual interest," and confesses
herself a " meliorist." She kept her passionate
interest in life until the end, and was always ready
to read about a new subject, learn a new language,
or set off on a new voyage. She and Lewes were
now received almost everywhere. At least, in

married and elderly society. At a dinner given
to them by Mr. (afterwards Lord) Goschen, there
were the Crown Prince of Germany and his wife,
the Dean of Westminster, the Bishop of Peter-
borough, Lord and Lady Ripon, Kinglake,
Froude, etc. Royalty and the Church now knew
her : it was a splendid victory. But still her books
were not given to unmarried women, and the
Midletons, who lived near Marian at Godalming,
although they had Tennyson and *all* the local
celebrities at their parties, never asked her – how
could they, with marriageable daughters ? Mr.
George Smith's daughter, too, was not allowed
to meet the great novelist until she married, but
hardly was she returned from her honeymoon
than she was rushed off to the Priory and presented. " So this is Dolly," George Eliot said in
her deep voice with a smile, and " Dolly " smiled
nervously back.

The delights of Witley were lessened by
Lewes' failing health. He had worn himself
out in George Eliot's service, and until the last
he was doing her errands still, helping her with
her collection of satirical essays (*Theophrastus
Such*), sending off the manuscript to Blackwood,
singing solos to her guests, reading letters and
opening parcels. As his health declined, George
Eliot hurried him round the country seeking
changes of air, but in vain ; presbyopia had
martyred him for many years ; now the end was
near, and on November the 28th, 1878, he died.

George Eliot was heartbroken. For twenty-five

years he had been her solace and guide, and they had meant all in all to each other. Never was marriage so united as this liaison, never did two human beings live more devotedly in wedlock than these two in sin. For some time after his death she was utterly shattered, and her excessive grief is reminiscent of that of Prince Albert's widow, whose mourning was the pattern and model of all Victorian devotion. She would see no one, do nothing ; Charles alone would she admit to her presence. She read no letters and wrote none, but one work she began to do as strength and energy returned : she set about arranging Lewes' unfinished manuscript. After two months of moping she was in a sadly weak and ill state, but was comforted by a visit from Sir James Paget, her doctor, who prescribed for her, and by the end of January 1879 she was writing to John Cross that she still wanted to live " a certain length of time," that she might do "certain things for His sake." Blackwood insisted on publishing *Theophrastus* and, although she considered it indecently soon after Lewes' death, she allowed it to appear in May, provided it were prefaced by a note saying it had been written for more than a year. Gradually she began to write letters ; to Elma Stuart she says : " I want you to know that He used the beautiful walking-stick in the last days," and by March, Gertrude and the children, Mrs. Congreve and Mrs. Burne-Jones were asked to tea. She made arrangements with Henry Sidgwick and Sir

Michael Foster to found a " George Henry Lewes " studentship in science, at Cambridge, and after some time the first student was chosen. On the 22nd April she wrote to John Cross – whom she had already promised should see her " sooner than anyone else " – " I am in dreadful need of your counsel. Pray come to me when you can, morning, afternoon or evening." He came at once : and from that time forward was with her constantly. His mother had died recently – her husband had recently died. It was a case of " Woman, behold thy . . . husband," " Son, behold thy mother." Motherhood was a deep instinct with George Eliot, but there was one deeper ; and when, after reading Dante together for less than a year, in April 1880 John proposed, she accepted. *Theophrastus* had been selling well, although we now regard it as exceedingly dull ; indeed the year 1879 had been full of blessings, though they were sadly tempered by ill-health, and a dreary eight weeks' illness. George Eliot had moved to Witley in the beginning of May 1879 and she never returned to the Priory. Her marriage to Mr. Cross took place on May 6th, 1880, a fortnight only after his proposal. It was a strange union, this mating of the sexagenarian, ugly, frumpish woman with a smart, rich, well-preserved man some twenty odd years her junior, who, although he was intelligent, had perhaps a somewhat muddled mind. His chief work, apart from his careful compilation of Marian's letters, was a book entitled *Some Impressions of*

Dante and the New World and some Aspects of Bi-metallism. He only died recently.

Many of Marian's lifelong friends were terribly shocked and disillusioned by her marriage, but the Cross family welcomed her with open arms. Lewes' son himself gave her away, and entirely approved of the match; but, best of all, it brought about a reconciliation with her family. Isaac Evans wrote to her after two and a half decades of silence, and George Eliot could feel she had at last attained tradition. It was for this she married and with her marriage she re-entered regularity, she ceased to be exceptional, she wiped out the ignominy of the past years. Cross did what Lewes never could do, he "made an honest woman of her." To her, as to all her class and most of her generation, marriage was a blessing for which to thank Heaven fasting, and Marian does not conceal her joy. "All this is a wonderful blessing to me, beyond my share, after I thought that my life was already ended and that, so to speak, my coffin was ready for me in the next room. I am able to enjoy my newly reopened life." And she writes rapturously of the joy of feeling daily "the loveliness of a nature close to one." She had been more reticent about her feelings for Lewes – one feels her letters after her marriage are almost too blatantly triumphant; she must announce her success to all and sundry, must "rub it in," emphasise it. Yet it was no love match, nor are her letters love letters, only triumph hymns. (In all her books the only love

letters are written by Casaubon.) It was, however, psychologically completely satisfying; she
basks in the love with which she is once more
surrounded. On her honeymoon she was physically magnificently well – went sightseeing, took
long walks, went to theatres, concerts, wrote
long letters, read widely. It was John who
succumbed (malicious Victorian rumour had it
that he tried to commit suicide on their wedding-
night!), and he grew quite ill in Venice, to recover
only in the Tyrolese Alps. On their return she
was at first very well, but during the autumn at
Witley had a " fresh onset of the kidney trouble "
that had "nearly carried her off the year before."
During October she was obliged to stay in her
bed, but read and talked no less for it. She began
her day's reading always with some chapters from
the Bible – the very Bible with big print that
Lewes had given her " in provision for her old
age." But Lewes, although he " saw no harm
in her reading it," had never shared her passion
for the Holy Book ; now she and John could enjoy
the Scriptures together, and this return, not to
the faith, but the background of her fathers, was
another added joy. In December she grew better,
and she and her husband moved to 4 Cheyne
Walk, where Dr. and Mrs. Congreve and Mrs.
Belloc visited them. On December 18th, Edmund
Gosse sat behind her at a popular concert in
St. James's Hall, and noticed how, in the chilly
room, she drew up and tightened round her
shoulders a woolly white shawl. Next day, a

Sunday, she had a slight sore throat, but was well enough to welcome Herbert Spencer, who brought her the news of Sir James Colvile's death. When he was gone, she sat down to write her condolences, but never finished the letter, and on the 22nd she herself, without a struggle, died. Her last words were " Tell them I have a great pain in the left side." She was buried in Highgate Cemetery, in the same grave as Lewes ; a Unitarian minister preached in the rain to the great gathering who accompanied her to her burial, ending his sermon with words from her poem, " O may I join the choir invisible."

CHAPTER XII

"WE have now," Miss Haldane says, "reached
a point at which it is right to consider George
Eliot as one of our classics, an artist and thinker
to be examined scientifically, without extrava-
gance or prejudice." At her death, the extrava-
gance came first ; for Acton, the " sun had gone
out," and Hale White wrote tearfully of the
" submarine deeps which she had sounded, into
which no plummet but hers had dropped,"
whilst others, less restrained, said that only
Shakespeare and Dante had any claim to stand
beside her – and they with one knee bended. She
represented completely the mid-Victorian era,
and it was small wonder that she excited the
enthusiasm she did. Her novels were read, not
only as literature, but as moral and æsthetic
teaching, and to find a parallel to her influence
we must wait for Bernard Shaw ; the attitude of
the Fabians to their leader has in it something
of the attitude of the intelligent public to George
Eliot during the latter part of her life, and immediately after her death. Hers were the only
novels the die-hards wished allowed in the newly
founded London Library, and she was taken as
an authority on almost any and every ethical
subject, although she herself, far clearer-minded,

more humble and more sane than her devotees,
never pretended to make any original contribu-
tions to speculative thought. Swiftly came the
reaction, and with it prejudice was substituted for
exaggeration. She was swept away in the general
spring cleaning which coincided with the birth of
a new century and the death of an old queen. As
duty, kinship, faith came to be regarded as
barriers to be surmounted, as complexes to be
overgot, so she grew more and more deserted,
until now she is to most people but a writer of
disagreeable holiday tasks, swallowed, but not
digested, skipped, rather than skimmed, in youth.
And those who write about her to-day are interested in the woman, not the writer, in the author,
not in her books. She is no longer even disliked ;
the gibes about her novels being " dictated to a
plain woman by the ghost of Hume," or of her
being " George Sand plus science and minus
sex," are heard no longer. Her psychology is
abhorrent to our psycho-analytical generation, her
dramas are purely intellectual to us – as passion-
less, as coldly classical as those of Corneille.
Frederick Harrison stated that it would be " the
duty of the more serious criticism of another
generation to revive her reputation as an abiding
literary force," and to determine what the final
judgment on her would be. To the accomplish-
ment of this duty there is one grave objection ;
that there can be no " final " judgment on any
historical or literary figure : each generation
revises the judgment of its predecessor ; every

year, every day, values and reputations are altered, sifted, often reversed. But we must grant George Eliot two enduring qualities : she is herself, historically, one of the most important figures in the social life of the mid-Victorian era, and her books are, historically, also invaluable guides to the Victorian attitude of mind. Ethically she has failed, because people will not for long suck unsugared pills, and the spiritless morality of *Felix Holt* and *Spanish Gypsy* has lost its effect, as, with the changing generations, moral values have changed. We do not ask to-day, as George Eliot did when "endeavouring to estimate a remarkable writer who aimed at more than temporary influence," whether he " animated long-known but neglected truths with a new vigour," nor yet whether he, " by a wise emphasis here, and a wise disregard there, gave a more useful or beautiful proportion to aims or motives." Her attempt to carry ethical purpose and erudition into art nearly destroyed that art : it was as though she had harnessed a racehorse to a plough and wondered that it broke down without moving the cumbersome instrument even a few yards. She subordinated Passion and Faith, Youth and Beauty, to Duty and Destiny, and used the loveliness of nature as illustrative of scientific fact. Such vivisection is odious to a generation which, in spite of the ghastly horrors of a world war, and the sordidness of a machine-laden universe, has learnt to worship in the ancient places. Yet George Eliot was a rebel in spite of

herself ; she denied her class, her traditions, her
education, her faith, her loyalties, yet in her heart
she kept and loved them still. And this contradiction in her makes her human to us, and makes her
readable : when we read the descriptions of the
country by this girl who left it, wilfully and
deliberately, to live in cities and suburbs, when
we know that the author of the homilies on the
sanctity of marriage, in *Romola*, herself lived in sin,
we are touched. There is a certain tragic dignity
about her as about those who " seek and cannot
find, who knock and to whom it is not opened,"
and we must feel sorry for this " quiet, anxious,
sedentary, serious, invalidish, middle-aged" lady,
without animal spirits, and without adventures or
sensations, who tried so hard to make bricks
without straw. Frederick Myers has compared
her with the emperor who summed up his view
of life in the words " *Nil expedit*," yet gave to his
legions, as his last watchword, "*Laboremus*," and
no comparison could be more just ; and he goes
on to describe in a magnificent passage of his
reminiscences a walk with her in the Fellows'
garden at Trinity, Cambridge, when she " pronounced with terrible earnestness how incon-
ceivable was God, how unbelievable immortality,
how peremptory and absolute was Duty."

Her writings have had many admirers and no
less detractors. It is true she had no sense of
form, and no love of, nor gift for handling, words,
nor much dramatic power, but she has an almost
unparalleled power of description, and her

characterisation is unequalled. Her people are all living, warm, vivid and human, her countryside is absolutely alive and real, and in no other novel are everyday things so solidified – one can cuddle her children and eat her apples, and smell her flowers as one can no one else's. Arnold Bennett considered that she will never be amongst the classical writers because her style is too rank, too " feminine in its lack of restraint, its wordiness, and the utter absence of feeling for form which characterises it." But it is difficult to deny a place amongst our classic authors to one who brought reality so successfully and completely into English literature. Her novels are not wholly first-rate ; they never have the grandeur of *The Idiot* nor the exquisiteness of *Northanger Abbey*; but so much of them *is* first-rate – nearly all *Adam Bede*, the first part of the *Mill*, the first part of *Silas Marner* and all of *Middlemarch* – that her place amongst the greatest of the Victorians is assured.

And, in spite of her faulty emphasis, she was so terribly in earnest that her emotions reach us, in spite of our instinctive suspicion of them. She let her sense of sin darken her life and her writings, she admitted herself to be " a luxurious person with an uneasy conscience," but, in the best moments of her life, her intuitive good sense and natural appetites triumphed over that middle-class intellect of hers. The best she has written is " of the earth, earthy," and as such will endure as long as the English countryside. Her immortality is thus assured, for it is derived whence Antæus drew his strength – from the " onlie begetter " of all earthly good.

BIBLIOGRAPHY

Acton, Lord : Article, " George Eliot," in *Nineteenth Century*. 1885.

Blind, Mathilde : *George Eliot*. Eminent Women Series. 1883.

Browning, Oscar : *George Eliot*.

Cooke, G. W. : *George Eliot : A Critical Study*. 1883.

Cross, J. W. : *George Eliot's Life and Letters*. Blackwood. 1885.

Early essays of George Eliot, privately printed. 1919.

Emily and Georges Romieu : *George Eliot*. Cape. 1932.

Gosse, Edmund : Article, " George Eliot," in *London Mercury*. 1919.

Haldane, Elizabeth : *George Eliot and Her Times*. Hodder & Stoughton. 1927.

Myers, F. W. : Article, " George Eliot," in *Century Magazine*. 1881.

Paterson, Arthur : *George Eliot : Family Life and Letters*. Selwyn & Blount. 1928.

Stephen, Leslie : *George Eliot*. English Men of Letters. Macmillan. 1902.